OPENING-UP
to your psychic self

by Petey Stevens

OPENING-UP to your psychic self by Petey Stevens. First copyright © in 1982 as THE PSYCHIC READER, Library of Congress catalog card number: TXu108-002. Second copyright © in 1983, OPENING-UP to your psychic self TXu-138-430.

FIRST EDITION; 1,000 printed, July 1983.
SECOND EDITION; 3,000 printed, December 1983.

ISBN 0-9612532-0-7

Jim Mascolo: principle typesetter, The Illustrated Word Type & Graphics
Lane Olsen: typesetter
Eric Schjeide: furniture maker (page 12, hand carved chair)
Petey Stevens: art overlay
All photographs taken by Scott McCue, professional photographer

---

Nevertheless Press
Box 9779
Berkeley, CA 94709

OPENING-UP
to your psychic self

This book is dedicated to

YOU

the SEEKER and the CREATOR

ACKNOWLEDGEMENTS

Writing and producing a book is a project that no one does completely alone. Because of this I would like to give my whole-hearted thanks to the following people.

I would especially like to thank my dear husband Rick. Thanks for all those hours that I needed to have you completely run our household and the school so that I could sit at my typewriter and create. Thanks for your love and belief in me.

Of course, my appreciation goes to my precious children who seemed to know and understand my need to write this book. Thanks Cassiopeia, Sarah, Solomon and Heather.

There are also my friends who gave me their helpful critical eyes and supportive hearts. Thanks Carla, Allen, Helene, and Vickie.

Many thanks go to the teachers that I have had, and the students that I have taught. It was through your sharing yourselves openly with me that I have come to understand psychic energy.

Finally my dearest thanks go to my parents, Carol and Bob Baldwin. Without your influence this book would never have been written.

TABLE OF CONTENTS

IV. APPENDIX

UNIT I
INTRODUCTION

THE PURPOSE OF THIS BOOK

Everyone is psychic! When you understand that the word psychic is derived from the Greek word *psychikos*, which means "of the Soul", you will realize that you are already psychic; for every Body on this planet Earth is created by and connected to their own Soul. When you become a student of the psychic realms, you are really experiencing your own psychic opening: you opening up to who you are, the TRUTH of your Soul manifested in your Body. This is a journey that once started you can never stop. Once you know the truth of who you really are, it is impossible to lie to yourself.

Each of you have a variety of different psychic abilities. Some of these abilities may be quite obvious to you right now such as precognition, (knowing who is on the phone when it rings) or telepathy (knowing what another is thinking). Other abilities may not seem like abilities at all: they may seem more like disabilities: such as when you take on another's emotions or another's thoughts you may assume that they are yours and run them through your Body. You will appear hysterical, out of control or confused. Still other abilities are so subtle that they seem to be hidden within you and may not be discovered until you become acutely aware of yourself and the world around you. An example of this is that you may be a sensitive receiver who is unconsciously and continuously programmed by subliminal messages from others or hyped-up advertisements. You really have to know yourself to be sure that when you make a decision or buy brand X that it is because you want to and not because you were programmed to do so!

This book will show you how to see and know your own abilities. It will show you how to see and know your own thoughts, opinions, judgments, and considerations so that you will not confuse them with another's. This book will show you how to read your own metaphors and symbolic messages. This book will also show you how to obtain your own psychic freedom. When you have invested yourself in another's way of thinking or being, then you are not free to be yourself. True freedom is when you have the ability to BE YOURSELF.

As you experience your psychic opening you may discover that your belief systems might be in conflict with the beliefs in this book. *"How can I see or hear a thought that belongs to another? Oh no, if I can see and hear another's thoughts, they must be able to see and hear mine!"* This will alter your perception of your reality. Your beliefs are no more than programming cards for your psychic computer (your personal psychic system). These programs can be changed by you. As you learn to use your Clairvoyance as a tool for seeing these cards and you develop the ability to manifest a change in them;

then you will begin to consciously create your own reality: as you like it!

The purpose of this book is to be a practical guide for your psychic opening. It is a workbook combining the introduction of concepts and the use of techniques and exercises. Yet it also includes enough metaphysics to challenge even the advanced student. Because the style is that of a workbook, it allows you to have autonomy and privacy during your personal psychic realizations. The concepts, vocabulary, explanations and exercises are introduced at appropriate points. They have been purposefully sequenced in a way that will produce a developmental experience of opening and understanding. By doing the exercises, learning the concepts and applying them to your every day life, you will obtain empirical evidence that you have psychic abilities. Your own subjective experiences provide you with a context for understanding this material. You will learn that your Clairvoyance can be a tool for seeing yourself and others clearly. For some this is extremely healing.

Most of my younger years I did not know that I and everyone else was psychic. My awakening to this realization came slowly, unfolding over many years. In retrospect, I see now that I was always psychic: wide open and out of control. My greatest psychic ability was to me and everyone else a disability: I could feel and become another's thoughts and emotions. This got me into a great deal of trouble, because neither I nor anyone around me recognized and diagnosed this as an open and out of control psychic ability. I appeared to be overemotional and unpredictable, and I was treated as such. I felt misunderstood and became quite rebellious towards the authority figures around me who assumed that they knew what was best for my well being.

I have worked very hard to clearly see and understand this part of myself. My struggle towards self-realization has become a great tool for me as a teacher. It allows me to have real life experiences on which to draw for understanding and compassion while teaching and guiding others through their own psychic openings. I truly believe that if I can clearly discover, see, realize and develop myself as a psychic human being, that anyone can!

Because my husband and I believe in the psychicness of all, we co-founded, co-created, and continue to co-direct Heartsong, a Clairvoyant Reading and Healing School in Berkeley, California. We started Heartsong in 1976 with one student in our living room. Since then Heartsong has become an entity unto itself. It serves the community with free healings, inexpensive psychic readings, one day workshops, beginning classes, advanced intensive programs and a professional training program. All services and classes stress freedom and autonomy within the opening process.

Heartsong has touched the lives of thousands of people. The students have ranged in age from eighteen to eighty years old. They come from all walks of life: different ethnic and religious backgrounds, different interests and vocations; some are rich and some are poor. What they have in common is a desire to experiment and explore, and a willingness to share and transform.

When students go through the opening process in one of Heartsong's advanced programs, they commit themselves to three sessions a week for a number of months. The psychic techniques are practiced over and over again until the students have integrated them into their every day lives. All of the exercises in this book have been used with Heartsong students for this purpose, and have proven themselves to be effective and helpful in teaching Clairvoyant Reading and Psychic Healing as vehicles for personal transformation and enlightenment.

HOW TO USE THIS BOOK
MOST EFFECTIVELY

This book was written very simply. It combines structure for teaching the beginner, practice for the intermediate, and a reminder for the advanced students. I will suggest that you read each concept through and notice what you think and how you feel about it. (Does it seem silly? Does it threaten your reality? Does it frighten you?) Then read the exercises through, and do them. You can leave the book open to the page of the exercise that you are doing, have a friend read them to you, or use the order form at the end of the book for cassette tapes of these exercises. In doing the exercises, you will really learn the concepts and techniques.

A simple mental image outline of a heart will be used as a psychic tool or point of focus. It will serve as a reminder that you are to be in affinity with yourself, accepting yourself as who you are with no judgments to get hung up on. Whenever you see three periods "..." you are to pause during the exercise and take time to reflect on the concept or lesson you are learning. There are occasional half pages and whole pages blank for you to fill in with your personal notes and reminders.

To truly understand the psychic realm, you must experience it. These exercises give you that experience. Repeat many times the exercises with which you have the most trouble. Each time you will understand more and see more. As with any art or talent: the more you practice, the better you get!

Clairvoyance works on an *"I see and understand you because I see and understand myself"* basis. Therefore, the first part of this book will teach you how to look at and see yourself. The second part of this book will teach you how to see and understand the WHOLE: you, me, and everyone else; all that we are together.

When used, **OPENING UP** will demystify the psychic world for you, teaching you how to "see" for yourself. It is my deepest desire that you find as much joy within the purity of your own self as I have found within opening up to myself.

Petey Stevens
Albany, California
1983

OPENING-UP
to your psychic self

Chapter One

TRANSCENDING YOUR BODY

THE MULTI-DIMENSIONAL "I"

The most desirable state of being is the integration of your parts into one-whole-you. However, to understand yourself, you must first understand the parts that make up the self.

The Elements. The physical elements of the Earth which organically make up each cell in your body. Each element has a consciousness alone and organized within a group of elements becomes the consciousness of an individual cell in your Body. *The elements of your birthsign create direction here: Earth, Air, Fire, Water.*

The Body. This not only includes the groups of cells working together creating their shared consciousnesses as parts of the Body (organs, glands, blood, hair, eyes, nails, brain, etc.) but also the parts of the Body personality: survival (instincts), expression (emotions) and reason (mind), each having their own individual consciousness. *Your genetic programming creates direction here.*

The Soul. The consciousness of the WHOLE of your Body and the life force therein. The consciousness and awareness of the Levels and parts within the whole of all we are together. *Your will creates direction here.*

The Oversoul. At this level you are the essence of all
that is. This is where you begin to be conscious of
the interconnectedness of all that exists: the oneness.
The God within creates direction here.

When I first studied the psychic, I identified myself with "I" the Body. At that time I thought that
my Soul was something outside of myself, surreal
and unattainable. At best I would experience it after
death. As I opened up to my responsibility as a
human form, I realized that I would have a broader
view if I were to be "I" the Soul sitting in and experiencing my Body.

#1 EXERCISE
The Parts of Yourself

Sit in a straight-backed chair with your hands and feet apart.

Close your eyes.

Let your mind flow. Notice which part of yourself you identify with. Which parts do you call *my--* and which do you call *I?* Simply think about each dimension: the Element, the Body, the Soul, the Oversoul. As with all the exercises in this book, use no effort. . . Just allow yourself to relax and notice what is going on within you and outside of you. Trust what you see, feel, hear, know or sense to be true.

End the exercise by bending your head and upper torso over your knees, allowing yourself to bring blood into your head and also to let go of any tensions caught in the back of your neck.

BEING IN A BODY

All of the abilities that are mentioned in this book are to be used in conjunction with your Body. To meet your full potential you must take care of your Body by answering the four basic maintenance needs:

1. **adequate nutrition.** Whether you are a vegetarian or a meat eater, you need enough protein to build and rebuild your body. You need enough carbohydrates to give yourself energy. Eating a variety of raw fruits and vegetables will give you the vitamins and minerals that you need. Fats and oils for vitamin and mineral absorption are also important. And lastly you need water (fluids). Every human being is different. Each has their own personal nutritional needs. Notice how you feel physically when you eat certain foods or leave out certain foods from your diet. Be sure that your diet is balanced so that you are not neglecting the total health of your Body.

2. **exercise.** To maintain a sense of order, and to keep the cells of your Body working as one unit, you need to exercise. Physical exercise helps to maintain a balance of intake and

excretion for all of your body parts. What type of exercise and how much time you spend doing it is decided by your wants, needs and likes.

3. **rest.** There has to be a time of day when every cell in your Body relaxes, when you let go of the tensions that you are holding onto. There needs to be a time of rejuvenation, renewal, a time for your organs to rest, a time for self healing. As with the foods that you eat and the exercises that you do, your own need for and type of rest is determined by you.

4. **breath.** As you breathe in air, not only are you feeding and nourishing every cell in your Body with oxygen, but you are also pulling in life force energy that you share with every other form of life on the planet. The air that you breath has no political, social, economic, religious or sexual preferences.

#2 EXERCISE
Breath and Body

Sit in a straight-backed chair.

Close your eyes.

Be aware of the way you are breathing. . . Pull
air in through your mouth into your lungs. . .
Fill your lungs up from the bottom up to the
top, pulling in nurturing oxygen and release
the wastes by exhaling from the bottom to the
top. Below and underneath your ribs should
expand as you inhale and contract as you
exhale. Breathe this way for a few minutes
until you have set up a rhythm between the
inhaling and the exhaling. At this point place
your breathing on automatic.

Notice how much exercise you have gotten so far
today. . . Have you been sitting all day?. . .
Or have you walked?. . . Has it been balanced
with enough rest?

What foods have you eaten today?. . . Did you
eat proteins, carbohydrates, oils, fruits and
vegetables?

How does your Body feel?. . .

Come out of trance.

Bend the upper part of your Body over your
legs, allowing all that pure oxygen that you
have been breathing to flow into your brain.

WHAT IS A TRANCE STATE?

Out of all the vocabulary within the explanation of psychic phenomena, the word *trance* seems to have the most spooky ideas attached to it. There seems to be fear that you will be controlled somehow or taken over by some great beast. It is simply not true. It may be helpful to you to associate the word *trance* with the word *transcend*, which means to be separate from or beyond the physical plane. The word trance as used in this book means a state of altered consciousness as gained through great concentration. The transcending occurs when your consciousness has moved from *I* the Body into *I* the Soul. Your Body does not disappear even though you are not identifying with it. Only your perspective has changed. Within this view, you are free from the dualism of the Body, the left-right, black-white, right-wrong type of thinking that keeps you stuck in either one or the other. Because your new perspective gives you a more objective view, it is easier to see the truth about who you are and why you have your particular style of functioning. Within this state of consciousness it is much easier to change yourself because you are no longer attached to what you want to change.

Human beings love habit patterns. This new way of looking at yourself might frighten different parts of you. When you feel fear or anxiety, or when you hear yourself say that *"This is silly, this is crazy, I can't do this,".* . . you are experiencing your resistance to change. All this chatter appears to be real to you. As a biological and psychic computer, you have run off of these programs for years. Some are made up from your feelings or thoughts, some are the opinions of others. To create a safe space for yourself while you open up psychically, you must give yourself, your Body, extra attention and the knowledge that opening up to who you are can and will give you a richer, more expansive life.

HOW TO GO INTO TRANCE

All the exercises in this book are done from a trance state. The exercises that you have done so far were done from a very light trance. Some of the exercises that you use later on in this book will need more concentration. Therefore, you will be in a deeper trance.

There are three meditative positions that are appropriate for you to use. One is to sit on the floor with your legs folded and crossed. The second is to lie down, flat on your back, on the floor or on a bed. The third position is the best one for most of the work that you will do in this book. It is to sit in a straight backed chair with your hands and feet apart. . . your hands on your lap, palms facing down, and your feet flat on the floor.

As you do the exercise start to be aware of how you get your information. Do you feel it, experience it, hear it, see it, or know it? After you have acknowledged the information, do you try to change it, or ignore it? Do you believe it? Start to be aware of who you are and how you react to trance.

When you are done with any given exercise it is important to give a definite ending. This is done by bending your upper torso and head over your lap. This will bring blood and oxygen into your head and will help release any tensions in your neck. Remember that if a part of your Body starts to hurt during a trance exercise, usually this is a hint as to where you are blocked and need more work.

#3 EXERCISE
Trance and Body Reactions

Sit in your trance position.

Close your eyes.

Go into trance.

Notice the thoughts you are having about going
into trance. Listen to yourself. . . Notice what
your feelings are about going into trance. . .

Communicate with yourself about your reasons
for wanting to open up psychically. . .what
you will gain from it. . .how it will affect
your life.

From a place of deep love, remind yourself that
you are in this as one unit and that you plan
to co-operate and co-create as *one* you. Pull
yourselves together within your Body and own
it — *I am*. After all, no one else has to live in
that Body but you!

Still from the center of your head, ask your Body
what it wants. And then ask what it needs. . .
Listen to yourself.

Come out of trance.

Bend over.

TWO NEW VIEWPOINTS

There are mainly two psychic viewpoints that you have of yourself and your reality. One is to be *in the center of your head.* This space is the free-est space in your Body. It is at the pineal gland and nestled in your memory banks. From this space you will have a clearer understanding of yourself. The other view is one from *up in the corner.* This out of Body view is even more objective than from the center of your head. Often when you go up in the corner to look at yourself, you will gain an overview of yourself and those around you.

For some of you this will be nearly impossible at first. The idea of going up in the corner may be threatening or ridiculous. Others of you may find yourself partially up there in the corner; you may feel compelled to keep returning yourself to the center of your head to question the reality of the *up in the corner* viewpoint. Still others will find it relatively simple. Repeat the exercise until you are comfortable with it.

#4 EXERCISE
The Center of Your Head

Sit in a straight-backed chair with your hands
   and feet apart.
Close your eyes.
Relax. . .notice that there is an exact geograph-
   ical center of your head. . .place your attention in the center of your head. . .there is a
   silvery blue light at the exact center of your
   head. . .this is the essence of your Soul. . .be
   that silvery blue dot of light. . .be in the
   center of your head.
Come out of trance.
Bend over.

#5 EXERCISE
Up In the Corner

Sit in your trance position.

Close your eyes.

Be in the center of your head.

Go into trance.

Make a strong affinity connection with your Body by using the thread of light that is attached to the dot of light and the center of your head.

Remind your Body of your deep desire to try something completely new. Remind your Body that you love it.

With your eyes open, choose a ceiling corner in the room—close your eyes and go up in the corner . . . pull yourself entirely up in the corner. Notice the silver cord of light that is at tached to you and goes from you in the corner to the crown of your Body's head . . . Notice your Body sitting in the chair. Notice how you feel when you are up in the corner.

Now be in the center of your head. . .pull yourself back into the center of your head. Notice how you feel when you are in the center of your head.

Now be up in the corner again. . .pulling
yourself up in the corner. . .pulling all of
yourself into that corner.

And be in the center of your head. . .bring all
of yourself into the center of your head.

Come out of trance.

Bend over.

WHAT YOU CAN EXPECT

As you look at yourself from these new viewpoints, you will notice that your Body and physical reality are governed by the laws of Time and Space. Time measures the duration of your appearance in physical form in the Physical World. It's measured in minutes, hours, days, weeks, months, years and lifetimes. Space measures the physical area that your Body occupies, where it is located and the movement it makes. These time and space limits give you a chance to develop one facet or aspect of your Soul while in a particular Body during a particular lifetime.

The Psychic World is of the Soul and does not have the same laws as that of the physical world. You can be in the past, the present or the future regardless of the time or space that your Body occupies. You can pass from one place to the other within moments. And you will see that the past will show you who you were and why you are in your present existence. The future will show you who and what you will probably be based on present tendencies. The precise moment in time where you have your full power is this present moment: The time in which, and Body to which, the silver cord is attached.

Beside the laws that govern movement and

duration, there is a new language to learn: The language of energy.

UNDERSTANDING ENERGY

All things in the Universe are made up of energy. Energy is the creative matter from which we create every part of our entire reality. Therefore everything around you is energy. Each particle of energy is moving at a different speed or vibration. Some energy moves so slowly that it can be perceived by your physical senses. You are holding this book with your physical hands, and you see the words on this page with your physical eyes. However, to truly understand what I am saying, you have to pick up the thoughts and images around the words. The energy of my thoughts and images moves at a much faster vibration than the written words, and although they are still hovering around the words, they cannot be seen by your physical eyes. Thoughts and images are seen by your Spiritual eye. Although a seer of this psychic energy is called a Clairvoyant, we all might as well be called Clairvoyants because we all have a Spiritual part of ourselves, and we all have potential Spirit Vision.

The true wonder of this energy is not in the phenomenon of the vision. The magic of this energy is when it is translated into information for intimate communication and for the understanding of yourself, others and eventually GOD (our collective consciousness).

The Principles of Energy

There are two main aspects of energy: the Male principle, and the Female principle. Whether you are a man or a woman, you have a need for both principles of energy. Without their interaction with each other there would be no life as you know it. It is the constant movement of their combined powers that creates you and your reality. The amount of Male and Female energy necessary to create any given manifestation is purely arbitrary. For you the amounts and balance of these energies changes at will within the normal daily expression of yourself.

When needed these energies are drawn into you from their collective pools. The Male principle lies deep within the Cosmos and the Female principle is within the Earth.

The following list mentions some of the attributes of these two principle parts of energy.

FEMALE	MALE
Earth	Cosmos
left	right
akali	acid
yeilding	firm
receptive	aggressive
achievement	action
holds and retains power	acts power
wisdom	movement
receiving	giving
draws into itself	repels
magnetic	electric
negative	positive
yin	yang

6 EXERCISE
Female and Male Principles

Sit in your trance position.

Close your eyes.

Be in the center of your head.

Go into trance.

As you breathe in air, relax and allow yourself to be here. Take full responsibility for your energy. This can be done by affirming and reaffirming your desire to be responsible for yourself. . . *"I am fully responsible for who I am. . . I am fully responsible for my energy."*

Allow yourself to have both Male and Female energy within your Body. . . Notice the dichotomies that these two forces create within you. . . Notice the degree of balance, or imbalance. Give yourself permission to have and be your own combined Male and Female self.

Be in the center of your head.

Come out of trance.

Bend over.

The Qualities of Energy

The meeting and interaction of the Male and Female principles of energy produce and form certain patterns of energy that have qualities unique to that particular meeting. As you personally experience these qualities, you consciously or unconsciously (subconsciously) translate them into information that you understand. In this way you read the energy.

Balance The evolutionary movement of any particular energy is measured within four states of dynamic balance and activity: structural, vibrational, directional, transformational.

Temperature implies the use or non-use of energy. Hot would tell you that the energy is being used and cold would tell you that the energy is not being used.

Shape will show you the limits of the energy. This is how you distinguish one pattern of energy from another.

Weight shows you the quantitative amount of energy that is not in movement. Heavy signifies a large amount of non-moving energy. Conversely, light signifies a small amount of non-moving energy.

Viscosity is determined by the internal interaction of the energy. It shows you what degree of fluidity that particular interaction of energy has.

Tone is the sound that the interaction makes: the sound of the energy. There are weak sounds and strong sounds signifying the power of the interaction.

Color represents certain characteristics that are attributed to the human nature. The chart that follows has been simplified, giving you four shades of each color. As you become familiar with translating color into meanings, you will be able to understand any color of energy that you could ever see.

COLOR	SHADE	CHARACTERISTIC ATTRIBUTES
BLACK	BLACK	EXTREME NEGATIVITY, FROZEN ENERGY
	DARK GREY	DEPRESSION, APATHY, LOSS
	GREY	CONFUSION
	SILVER	POWER
BROWN	DARK BROWN	NEGATIVITY, MALICIOUSNESS
	BROWN	GROUNDEDNESS
	LIGHT BROWN	EARTHY
	COPPER	HARMONY WITH THE PLANET
RED	WINE RED	NEGATIVE EMOTIONS, HATE, ANGER
	RED	PASSION, STIMULATION
	ROSE PINK	HOPE, OPTIMISM, CHEERFULNESS
	PINK	LOVE
ORANGE	BURNT ORANGE	HYSTERICAL EMOTIONS, MISCHIEVOUSNESS
	ORANGE	CREATIVITY
	LIGHT ORANGE	VITALITY, HEALING
	PEACH	NURTURING LOVE
YELLOW	MUSTARD YELLOW	MANIPULATIVE, COWARDICE
	DARK YELLOW	INTELLECTUALIZING, RATIONALIZING
	YELLOW	INTELLIGENCE, QUICK WIT
	LIGHT YELLOW	WISDOM, LIGHT
GREEN	DARK GREEN	GREED, JEALOUSY
	FOREST GREEN	GROWTH
	LIGHT GREEN	CALM, QUIET, PEACEFUL
	TORQUOISE	HUMOR, PLAYFULNESS
BLUE	DARK BLUE	FANATICISM, SERIOUSNESS
	ROYAL BLUE	DEVOTION, ROYALTY
	SKY BLUE	CLARITY
	SILVER BLUE	CERTAINTY
PURPLE	DARK PURPLE	DOGMATIC
	INDIGO	RELIGIOUS
	PURPLE	COMPASSION
	LIGHT PURPLE	COMPASSION
VIOLET	LAVENDER	SELF—ESTEEM
	VIOLET	ENTHUSIASM
	LIGHT VIOLET	HIGH ASPIRATIONS
	ULTRA LIGHT VIOLET	SPIRITUALITY
WHITE	WHITE	PURITY
GOLD	WHITE GOLD	SUPREME POWER
	YELLOW GOLD	SUPREME INTELLIGENCE
	PINK GOLD	SUPREME LOVE

#7 EXERCISE
Color

Sit in your trance position.

Close your eyes.

Be in the center of your head.

Go into trance.

Allow yourself to relax. . .

To understand color you must experience it.
Postulate that enery cell in your Body is red
. . .feel that red, see that red, know that red,
be that red. . . Spend several minutes on each
color, feeling, seeing, knowing and being. . .
allow every cell in your Body to understand
each color. Trust your own information:

orange

yellow

green

blue

purple

violet

gold

Be in the center of your head.

Come out of trance.

Bend over.

Translating the Qualities of Energy

Each person on the planet is different. In any given energy situation, you and the others will choose different qualities to *see*. You might react more to color while another might react more to the tone, or to shape. Go with your gut feelings! When you sense something about the energy, TRUST YOURSELF. Believe in what you *feel, hear, see,* or *know* about the situation.

Chapter Two

ENERGY CIRCUITRY

GROUNDING CORD
ENERGY CHANNELS
HOW TO RUN YOUR ENERGY
USE OF COLORS
DURING TRANCE STATES

ENERGY CIRCUITRY

You have specific circuitry and channels for running energy into and through your Body. These psychic hook-ups feed and nurture your entire energy system, send communication to and within the parts of your system and transport wastes from your energy system. They appear as pipes or conduit and have specific and necessary functions.

GROUNDING CORD

Before you begin practicing psychic work, you must establish a strong connection into the planet. This connection goes from the base of your spine into the center of the Earth, and it is called your *Grounding Cord.* It has three main functions.

1. Your Grounding Cord is a statement of commitment to your Body, the Planet Earth and the reality you are experiencing. It is an energy connection that keeps you in your Body when emotions are heavy and problems are many. It helps you to be responsible for your actions and reactions towards the situations and people in your every day life.

2. Most people forget that it is quality and not quantity that gives them their freedom and power, so they pull into their Bodies more energy than they

need to function at their full potential. This excess, if not released through the Grounding Cord, will blow out or burn out the Energy Body and eventually the Physical Body. Your Grounding Cord will stabilize your energy by releasing your excess energy into the center of the Earth.

3. The last and equally important function that your Grounding Cord has is to release wastes: not only the psychic wastes you accumulate, but also the wastes that others dump into you (anger, insults, opinions, judgments, etc.). It is hard enough to balance your own energy: it is impossible to try to balance yours and another's in your own Body. Just as a particular T.V. channel can only receive the transmitted waves of that particular channel, you can only use *your* energy in *your* Body. Another's energy kept too long within you will hurt you.

Once you establish your Grounding Cord, you will find everything that you do, in or out of trance, easier.

#8 EXERCISE
Grounding

Sit in your trance position.

Close your eyes.

Be in the center of your head.

Go into trance.

Breathe deeply. . .until you are relaxed and settled into your chair. Be at one with yourself.

Place your attention in your pelvic cradle at the base of your spine. . . Now with every breath that you breathe in, postulate that you are drawing into your pelvic cradle long threads of golden energy. Reach into the very depths of your Soul for this energy. . . As these threads meet they become fused into a long golden rope and rolled into a large ball. . . Feel the power and strength of that energy. . . Allow a portion of that golden twined energy to drop down between your legs. . . and gather it into a small dense ball of 14 karat gold still attached to the golden twine that is still in your pelvic cradle. . . Now with every exhalation of your breath, allow that weighted gold ball to drop down into the center of the Earth. . .all the way down to the exact center of the Earth. . .so that there is a golden energy beam from the base of your spine to the center of the Earth.

Place your attention at the base of your spine and follow your Grounding Cord through the layers of the Earth: rock, water, gasses, minerals, molten lava, into the iron core heart of the Earth. . . Allow your weighted, golden ball to fuse with the iron core of the Earth. . . giving you a permanent attachment to the Planet Earth. . . When this happens you will feel a slight shift in your energy, a sense of being relaxed and here in the present moment.

Leave your Grounding Cord down. . .

Be in the center of your head.

Come out of trance.

Bend over.

ENERGY CHANNELS

The main Energy Channels are located within your spinal column. Messages, wastes and nourishment pass through these Channels with surprising integrity. The messages travel as imprints of ideas. The wastes travel as fragmented pieces of your energy and other people's energy. The nourishment travels as life force *kundalini* energy, a combination of Earth and Cosmic energies.

The following picture will give you an idea of where your main Energy Channels are.

#9 EXERCISE
Energy Channels

Sit in your trance position.

Close your eyes.

Be in the center of your head.

Go into trance.

Ground yourself.

Place your attention on the arches of your feet.
Postulate that there are openings in the arches
of your feet. . . You may open them like the
iris of a camera. . . Follow your attention up
the calves of your legs and your thighs. . .
Your two leg Channels meet at the base of
your spine. . . Allow your attention to go up
your spinal column to the crown of your
head. . . At the crown of your head, open up
again like the iris of a camera. . . Allow your
Channels to be real and open. . . You might
feel a slight sensation or tingling in your Body
as you place your attention on these Channels.

Be in the center of your head.

Come out of trance.

Bend over.

HOW TO RUN YOUR ENERGY

If you are tired, frequently getting sick, unable to feel your emotions, unable to express your power, unable to express yourself or often confused, then you are not running your energy correctly through your Body. When you are running your energy in the correct directions, hooked-up to the appropriate energy patterns, you can accomplish your full potential in any given situation because you will be exhibiting the greatest respect for your personal integrity, freedom and autonomy.

You are bringing two energies into your Body: Earth energy from the Earth and Cosmic energy from the Cosmos (Universe). It is essential that you only bring energy from your own essense into your Body and through your Channels because it is yours and is totally correct for you. Never channel another's energy in order to nourish your Body because it would not nourish you: it would eventually weaken you and make you sick. You would lose your integrity and forget who you are. You would lose your freedom and not be yourself, and you would not be autonomous because you would be programmed by the other's energy.

Please be gentle with yourself. Too much energy brought in too fast can blow out or burn out these circuits because of the force created by an overload.

With your Grounding Cord open and attached to the Earth's core, you have a safety valve enabling excess energy to be released through it and into the Earth. The quality of the energy is more important than the quantity.

USE OF COLORS
DURING TRANCE STATES

Each time you run energy through your Body, you set a mood, disposition or mental state for yourself with the colors that you choose. These colors are determined by what you wish to experience. Therefore the choice is arbitrary.

For the sake of simplicity and teaching, I have chosen colors for the exercises in this book which I feel are appropriate. If you find any of these choices bad for you, change the colors of the Earth and Cosmic energies until you are satisfied.

#10 EXERCISE
Running Your Energy

Cosmic energy. . .gold
Earth energy. . .silver

Sit in your trance position.

Close your eyes.

Be in the center of your head.

Go into trance.

Ground yourself.

Recognize and acknowledge your Energy Channels. . .allow them to be open. . .

Place your attention at the arches of your feet and bring into your feet openings a silver Earth energy. . . Allow this energy to travel up your leg Channels and into your pelvic cradle. . . Hold this energy here for a moment. . .

Now place your attention on the crown of your head. . .from that opening bring into the crown of your head a gold Cosmic energy. . . Pull it down the back part of your back Channels and into your pelvic cradle.

Combine, balance and blend these energies within your pelvic cradle. . . Allow that mixture of Earth silver and Cosmic gold to go up the front part of your back Channels and out the crown of your head; never force it to move. . .allow the energy to flow through your energy Channels as if water. . .flowing

with the current of the Universe. . . Maintain
this energy flow for ten minutes.
Be in the center of your head.
Come out of trance.
Bend over.

#11 EXERCISE
Color Play

Sit in your trance position.
Close your eyes.
Be in the center of your head.
Go into trance.
Ground yourself.
Open your energy Channels.
Play with the colors on the color chart. . . Pull
different colors and/or combinations of colors
into your energy Channels. . . Earth and
Cosmic energy. . . What is your reaction to
the colors?. . .combine colors. . .different
colors. . .groups of colors. . . What combina-
tions of which colors cause what sensation
and feelings with you?. . . Discover which
colors make you happy and productive. . .
Which colors affect you negatively. . .
Allow yourself to have the colors that affect you
positively.
Be in the center of your head.
Come out of trance.
Bend over.

Chapter Three

SELF-REGULATING ENERGY PATTERNS

THE CHAKRAS

THE AURA

THE TWELVE LEVELS OF
CONSCIOUSNESS

THE GENETIC KEY

PICTURES

SELF-REGULATING ENERGY PATTERNS

Your personal energy system contains certain patterns of energy that define who you are by regulating how you bring yourself into and through your Body. These patterns of energy are stable or similarly positioned on all people. Your individuality is expressed because of the freedom you have in choosing what qualities of energy to run in your Body. Some people call your style of running energy through these patterns your personality because the style itself determines how you survive, feel, respond, love, communicate, understand, perceive, trust and create.

THE CHAKRAS

You have energy centers on your Body called *Chakras.* The word Chakra is a Sanskirt word that means wheel and is so named because from a front view a Chakra looks like a wheel. Each center transmits and receives energy messages in three ways:

intra-personally (within the self)
inter-personally (from one Body to another Body)
trans-personally (beyond the Body. . .one Soul to another Soul)

Due to styles of relating to one's own self and to others, all Chakras look and act differently. Because energy is in constant movement at different moments and in different situations, the same Chakra may have several ways in which it appears. Yet it is always located at the same region, and always has the same primary function.

You have twelve major Chakras. Seven are located *in the Body* and five are located *out of the Body*. The Body Chakras are each associated with a specific body region and a specific glandular or neural center of activity. They form the classical basis on which the Body organizes and processes perceptions, information and actions. It is through these centers that you send and receive personal energy messages. The *out of Body* Chakras are where you translate your ideas and belief structure to create and manifest the reality you experience, and where you unite and share with the WHOLE (everyone and everything that is) to create and manifest the Universe and beyond.

As you study your own Chakras, be aware of the attitudes and reactions that you have for each of them.

THE BODY CHAKRAS

Your seven major Body Chakras allow you to manifest your Soul self in the Body. The potential of each Chakra is determined by both your genetic programming and your early childhood experiential programming. Both of which you will learn to alter. Besides the seven Body Chakras, you also have smaller chakras in your feet and hands.

FIRST CHAKRA

Name: Survival Chakra, Root Chakra.

Location: Base of your spine.

Glands: Gonads, ovaries.

Analogy: Roots, toilet plumbing.

Functions: Grounding, releasing excess energy, reproduction, blends Earth and Cosmic energies; contains programming necessary to keep your Body alive, your personality intact, and your Soul attached to your Body.

Abilities: To be committed to yourself and your reality, to be connected to the Planet Earth, to let go, to produce healthy children, to satisfy your physical needs, physical balance and physical health, to know how to take care of yourself, to be responsible for yourself, good Body image.

Disabilities: "Freaking out", getting "blown-out", jumpy, alienated, unable to produce healthy children, pre-occupied with survival, unable to take care of yourself, drug and alcohol addiction, poor Body image.

#12 EXERCISE   Cosmic energy. . .copper
First Chakra   Earth energy. . .brown

Sit in your trance position.
Close your eyes.
Be in the center of your head.
Go into trance.
Ground yourself.
Run your energy.
Place your attention at the base of your spine. . .
  Postulate that you have a Chakra that is attached to the base of your spine at your back
  Channels, and it protrudes beyond and in front
  of your Physical Body about six inches. . . All
  the information that you could ever need about
  your Body is here.
Choose something about your Body that you
  want to change. . . In front of you place the
  outline of a heart. . . From your First Chakra,
  throw off that which you do not want. . .postu-
  late that the energy that you are throwing into
  the heart is exactly what you want to change
  from. . .see the heart take the energy in. . .
  When the heart is full and you are cleansed,
  postulate that the energy within the heart is
  neutralized.
Take that neutral energy in front of you and
  change it into the image of that which you

want. . . Bring it back into your Body by pulling it into your First Chakra and into your back channels, allowing every cell in your Body to be nourished by it. . . Allow the energy to fill up any places that are emptied by the first process of letting it go. . . Allow yourself to HAVE the change that you have initiated.

Be in the center of your head.

Be what you want to be!

Come out of trance.

Bend over.

SECOND CHAKRA

Name: Clairsentient Chakra (clear feeling).

Location: The center of your abdomen, below navel.

Glands: Spleen, pancreas.

Analogy: Radar.

Functions: To experience all levels of feeling (emotions, sensations, tactile, sexual), picking up the *vibes* (feelings) of another, socializing, Body communication, balance of Male and Female energy in the Body.

Abilities: To feel the full spectrum of your emotions clearly, and at your will, to be able to distinguish your emotions from the emotion's of other's, empathy, validation of another, physical intimacy, physical openness, balance, complementarity (drawing the other side for completion.)

Disabilities: Hysterical while acting out the emotions of others, controlled by sex, using sex to manipulate another, controlled by flattery, using flattery to manipulate another, sympathy (becoming the emotions or problems of another), no boundaries.

#13 EXERCISE
Second Chakra

Cosmic energy. . .sky blue
Earth energy. . .turquoise

Sit in your trance position.

Close your eyes.

Be in the center of your head.

Go into trance.

Ground yourself.

Run your energy.

Place your attention at the exact center of your abdomen. . . You will notice that your Second Chakra is here. . . Be sure that it is attached to your back spine and protrudes in front of your Body about six inches. . . This is your feeling center.

Outside and in front of your Second Chakra, place the outline of a heart. . . Choose a recent emotional experience that still upsets you and throw that experience into that heart. . . Drain from that experience the disturbing emotions. . . Now, by throwing them into that experience in front of you, try out different emotions within the context of that experience. . . When you find one that is most appropriate for you, allow it to stay in that experience. . . Pull the heart-experience and new emotions into your Second Chakra. . . Notice that you are in control of your emotions. . .any emotion that you cannot control is not yours. . . The next time you feel an uncontrollable emotion, send it down your Grounding Cord because it is not your energy. You can control your own energy; you cannot control another's energy in your Body.

Be in the center of your head.

BE YOURSELF.

Come out of trance.

Bend over.

THIRD CHAKRA

Name: Solar Plexus Chakra.

Location: Just below your sternum.

Glands: Adrenal glands, *neural center:* solar plexus.

Functions: Power center, energizes your Body by distributing vital life force energies to every part of your Body; expression of creativity through your Body, transmutes psychic energies into physical energies.

Abilities: To take responsibility for your energy, setting limits for yourself, being in control of your energy, self-starter, self-motivator, balance of giving and receiving, out of Body experience, to travel to the past or the future, to be in present time.

Disabilities : Having no energy, "Drained", inability to say *no*, sleepy, cannot finish projects, "untogether", unorganized, needing outside motivation from others, overeating, undereating, ego tripping, power tripping, controlled by fear (unable to move), being dogmatic, being stuck in the past or in the future.

#14 EXERCISE   Cosmic energy. . .light yellow
Third Chakra   Earth energy. . .light yellow

Sit in your trance position.

Close your eyes.

Be in the center of your head.

Go into trance.

Ground yourself.

Run your energy.

Just below your sternum you will notice your Third Chakra. . . It is attached to your back channels at your spine and protrudes about six inches in front of your Body.

Go up in the corner and look back down at your Body. . . Notice the distribution of energy throughout your Body. . . Where is most of your energy? Around your head? heart? feelings?. . . Do you want it there?. . . Are you satisfied with the distribution of your energy? If so, leave it alone! If not, postulate that you are changing portions of your energy to be where you want it. . . Take full responsibility and control of your own energy.

Be back in the center of your head.

Be your own power.

Come out of trance.

Bend over.

FOURTH CHAKRA

Name: Heart Chakra.

Location: At the center of your chest, near your heart.

Glands: Thymus.

Analogy: Synthesizer.

Functions: Affinity (to be at one with; to become one with), life expectancy, self-concept, keeps Body alive by drawing (affinity) the Soul to the Body.

Abilities: To be at one with yourself (all dimensions at one with the others), to be at one with another, to be at one with the Group of others, to be at one with a Group of others, to be at one with an idea, to be at one with the Planet to be at one with God, loving and accepting yourself, loving and accepting others, compassion, at peace with yourself, to reach in and "touch" another, to have what you want and need, trust, a sense of abundance or wealth.

Disabilities : To be at war with yourself, to be at odds with another, to experience hurt and pain about yourself, controlled by love, suicidal, acting "nice" and "loving" when you really do not feel it, *not* to have, a sense of emptiness.

#15 EXERCISE
Fourth Chakra

Cosmic energy. . .lavender
Earth energy. . .lavender

Sit in your trance position.

Close your eyes.

Be in the center of your head.

Go into trance.

Ground yourself.

Run your energy.

Notice your Heart Chakra. . . It is attached to your back channels at your spine. . . It protrudes about six inches in front of your Body.

Postulate that you the Element, you the Body, you the Soul, and you the Oversoul are all one. . . Pull yourself together as if each dimension of you has a body (Elemental Body, Physical Body, Astral Body, Spiritual Body) and that each of these bodies has a Heart Chakra. . . Juxtapose the Heart Chakras of each on top of each other. . . Allow the Chakras to be at ONE with each other. . . Allow these Bodies to synthesize into one. . . Be at one with yourself.

Be in the center of your head.

Love yourself.

Come out of trance.

Bend over.

FIFTH CHAKRA

Name: Throat Chakra.

Location: At your throat.

Glands: Thyroid.

Analogy: Radio.

Function: To communicate with another, to hear energy, clairaudience (to hear out of Body Spirits), telepathy.

Abilities: To express yourself verbally, to listen, to tone or sing, to hear Astral music, certainty in telepathy (giving and receiving thoughts), communication with parts of yourself (inner voice).

Disabilities : Confusion of all the voices within (other's thoughts, inner voice, Spirits), tuning others out (choosing to ignore by not hearing them), not able to express yourself, self-trashing (putting yourself down).

#16 EXERCISE
Fifth Chakra

Cosmic energy. . .light green
Earth energy. . .forest green

Sit in your trance position.

Close your eyes.

Be in the center of your head.

Go into trance.

Ground yourself.

Run your energy.

Notice your Throat Chakra. . . It is at your throat and hooked up at the top of your spine, and it protrudes about six inches in front of your Body.

Notice if you have any heat or color collected around your neck. . .these are unexpressed words that you have collected there. . . Drain the color out the front of your Throat Chakra. . . Do not be surprised when you become outspoken.

Notice the voices inside your own head. . . Choose and designate a certain tone to be your own inner voice, and start to recognize it when you hear it (the tone of the voice is arbitrary: pick soft, loud, high, low).

Be in the center of your head.

Come out of trance.

Bend over.

SIXTH CHAKRA

Name: Third Eye, Spirit Eye.
Location: In the center of your head.
Glands: Pineal.
Analogy: Television.
Functions: To see energy, to perceive and project reality.
Abilities: Clairvoyance (to see clearly), to see Spirits without Bodies, to see Auras and Chakras, to see and appreciate beauty, to have vision, to see into the past, to see into the probable and possible futures, to see all the energy formations and patterns mentioned in this book, to see mental image pictures, to be intelligent.
Disabilities : To see monsters and other lower energy levels, to be confused, not able to think in logical sequences, to be blind to beauty, over-rationalizing or over-intellectualizing problems.

#17 EXERCISE
Sixth Chakra

Cosmic energy. . .yellow gold
Earth energy. . .yellow

Sit in your trance position.

Close your eyes.

Be in the center of your head.

Go into trance.

Ground yourself.

Run your energy.

Notice that your Third Eye is hooked up into the center of your head at your back Channels, and it protrudes about six inches in front of your head.

From the center of your head, look through your Third Eye. . . Take a mental picture of a heart from inside your memory banks (the memory banks are located around and over you as you sit in the center of your head). . . Then place that heart in front of your Third Eye. . .look at it, return it to your memory banks. . . Now take an image of a tree and place it in front of you; look at it, and return it to your memory banks. . . Then in sequence take a flower, glass of water, house. . . After looking at these images be sure to file them back in your memory banks, or you will have to look at them all day long!

Take your arm and extend it in front of you. . .

Look at your hand. . . With your eyes closed, see an image of your hand. . .notice the colors and light shining around your hand. . .notice the difference between the mental images you looked at before, and the energy you just looked at.

Be in the center of your head.

Be in the present moment.

Come out of trance.

Bend over.

SEVENTH CHAKRA

Name:	Crown Chakra.
Location:	At the crown (top) of your head.
Glands:	Pituitary.
Analogy:	Opening flower.
Functions:	To know energy, to bring in Cosmic energy, to connect you to the Cosmos, to release excess energy and wastes.
Abilities:	To know without using reason, to have faith, connection with ALL INTELLIGENCE, trancemediumship (when the Soul of a particular Body leaves their Body and allows another Soul to run their Body).
Disabilities :	Having no faith, uncontrolled trance-mediumship, being controlled.

Please note:

Not all humans have trancemediumship hookups. If you feel that you do, please seek a professional psychic with high standards to aid you in either developing this ability or shutting it down.

#18 EXERCISE
Seventh Chakra

Cosmic energy. . .yellow gold
Earth energy. . .light yellow

Sit in your trance position.

Close your eyes.

Be in the center of your head.

Go into trance.

Ground yourself.

Run your energy.

Notice that your Crown Chakra is attached to the back Channels at the center of your head. . .feel the openness of the top of your head. . . The Chakra goes beyond your head about six inches . . .notice the energy flow. . .allow the energy to flow out the Crown Chakra with the smoothness of water.

From the center of your Crown Chakra, create a golden cord of energy and send it to the center of the Universe connecting you with ALL KNOWLEDGE, ALL INTELLIGENCE.

Be in the center of your head.

BE YOURSELF.

Come out of trance.

Bend over.

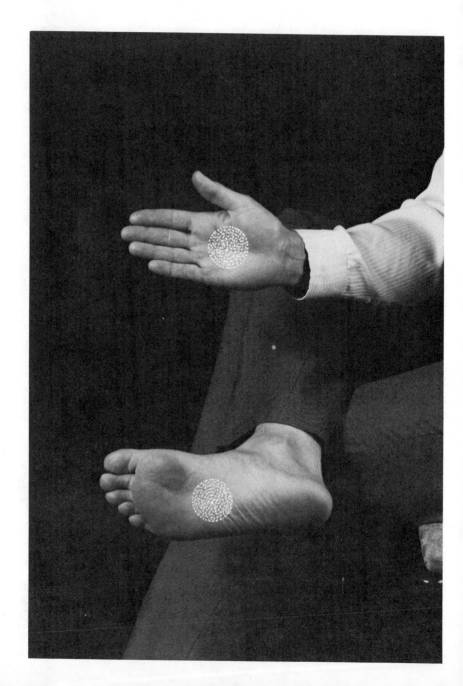

FEET CHAKRAS

Location: You have two of them, one in the bottom of each foot at the arch.

Functions: To bring in Earth energy.

Abilities: To make the Body real by bringing Earth energy into the Body, to dance, run, skate, ski. . .any creative movement of your feet, balance.

Disabilities : Foot problems, trip easily, left-right imbalance.

#19 EXERCISE   Cosmic energy. . .none

Feet Chakras   Earth energy. . .copper

Sit in your trance position.

Close your eyes.

Be in the center of your head.

Go into trance.

Ground yourself.

Place your attention on your Feet Chakras. . .
Open them. . .and pull in copper Earth energy. . . Feel the energy moving through your feet. . .experience it. . . . .

Be in the center of your head.

Come out of trance.

Bend over.

HAND CHAKRAS

Location: You have two, one in the palm of each hand.

Functions: To manifest creativity on the physical plane, Healing, Reading energy.

Abilities: To express oneself through art, music, building, healing, manifesting ideas, creating.

Disabilities : To hurt someone with your hands (too much energy) or not to use your hands for creative expression (too little energy).

#20 EXERCISE
Hand Chakras

Cosmic energy. . .light orange
Earth energy. . .orange

Sit in your trance position.

Close your eyes.

Be in the center of your head.

Go into trance.

Ground yourself.

Run your energy.

Place your attention on your Hand Chakras. . . open each of them up as the iris in a camera opens up. . . Make a cord of energy starting from the center of each Hand Chakra, moving up your arms, through your shoulders and into your Heart Chakra. . . Tap into your energy system here and allow your energy to flowdown your arms and out your Hand Chakras. . .these are your creative hook-ups.

Be in the center of your head.

Come out of trance.

Bend over.

OUT OF BODY CHAKRAS

All of the *out of Body* Chakras are bi-polar and work together in pairs to create and manifest both your personal Reality and the Reality that you share with all others. The upper Chakras, above your head, deal with the creative ideas, plans and blueprints of your individual and your shared Realities. Their lower counterparts deal with the gravity needed to pull the ideas into the physical plane and the physical matter needed to manifest those ideas.

There are five bi-polar *out of Body* Chakras. The first three are the *Creative Rings* of your personal Reality. The last two are the *Unity Rings* that you share with all other living Beings in this Universe and Beyond.

CREATIVE RINGS
EIGHTH CHAKRA

Upper Eighth—Cosmic Energy Regulator

Location: One foot above your head.

Function: To filter, purify and temper Cosmic energy to make it fit for your Body, to regulate the amount and color of the Cosmic energy.

Abilities: Correctness of energy for your Body, being in touch with the Cosmos.

Disabilities: To be owned by a self-proclaimed Guru, to be cut off from the Heavens.

Lower Eighth—Earth Energy Regulator

Location: One foot below your physical feet.

Function: To filter, purify, and temper Earth energy to make it fit for your Body, to regulate the amount and color of the Earth energy.

Abilities: Correctness of energy for your Body, being in touch with the Earth.

Disabilities: Cut off from the Earth, litterbug (no attachment or responsibility for Earth).

#21 EXERCISE   Cosmic energy. . .silver blue
Eighth Chakra   Earth energy. . .copper

Sit in your trance position.

Close your eyes.

Be in the center of your head.

Go into trance.

Ground yourself.

Run your energy.

Place your attention on your Earth energy Regulator and be there. . . Open the Chakra up and experience your oneness with the Planet Earth.

Now place your attention on your Cosmic energy Regulator. . . Open the Chakra up and experience your oneness with the Cosmos. . .

Be in the center of your head and experience your combined oneness with both the Earth and the Cosmos.

Be in the center of your head.

Come out of trance.

Bend over.

NINTH CHAKRA — PROBABLE UNIVERSE

Upper Ninth

Location: Three feet above your physical head.

Functions: Laboratory for creating your personal reality, to have a full scope of probabilities. Given your present situations, you experiment with different likely ways of being and having. Just as a scientist would mix and fill vials, you mix and color energy patterns until you get a clear image of what you want to create.

Abilities: To create new ways of Living and Being, openmindedness.

Disabilities: Stuck in a fantasy world of what could be rather than living in what is.

Lower Ninth

Location: Three feet below your physical feet.

Functions: Laboratory for manifesting your personal Reality (what is real to you), pull creations into Reality.

Abilities: Gravity.

Disabilities: To be crippled, unable to walk.

#22 EXERCISE
Ninth Chakra

Cosmic energy. . .orange

Earth energy. . .orange

Sit in your trance position.

Close your eyes.

Be in the center of your head.

Go into trance.

Ground yourself.

Run your energy.

Place your attention on your lower Probability Chakra. . . Open it up. . . Notice the nurturing magnetic quality of this Chakra. . . pulling to it and giving life. . .

Now place your attention on your upper Probability Chakra. . . Open it up. . . Notice the creative, never-ending pool of probabilities. . .

Be in the center of your head.

Come out of trance.

Bend over.

TENTH CHAKRA — POSSIBLE UNIVERSE

Upper Tenth

Location: Four feet above your physical head.

Functions: Laboratory for the creation of new and inventive ideas for your personal reality, having the full scope of possibilities.

Abilities: Future thinker, Sage.

Disabilities: Stuck in a fantasy world.

Lower Tenth

Location: Four feet below your physical feet.

Functions: Laboratory for manifesting and creating new combinations of matter for creating your personal reality.

Abilities: Molten lava. . .primal Elements.

Disabilities: To be physically paralized, unable to move.

#23 EXERCISE
Tenth Chakra

Cosmic energy. . .orange
Earth energy. . .light orange

Sit in your trance position.
Close your eyes.
Be in the center of your head.
Go into trance.
Ground yourself.
Run your energy.
Place your attention on the lower Possibility
    Chakra and open it up...Be at one with the
    creative matter of the Planet Earth.
Place your attention on your upper Possibility
    Chakra and open it. . . Be at one with the
    creative ideas of the Cosmos.
Be in the center of your head.
Come out of trance.
Bend over.

UNITY RINGS
ELEVENTH CHAKRA — UNIVERSAL CHAKRA

Location: Below your feet and above your head.
Function: Synthesize the Universe and all in it.
Abilities: Understanding the oneness of a group,
                   a non-ego state.
Disabilities: To have nothing in the physical reality,
                   no Body, "dead".

#24 EXERCISE
Eleventh Chakra

Cosmic energy. . .pink
Earth energy. . .rose pink

Sit in your trance position.
Close your eyes.
Be in the center of your head.
Go into trance.
Ground yourself.
Run your energy.
Be in the lower Universal Chakra and be the creative essence of the matter that makes up the Universe. . .
Be in the upper Universal Chakra and be the creative essence of the thoughts and ideas that make up the Universe. . .
Be in the lower Universal Chakra and be the matter that this Universe is made up of. . . notice how group creative thoughts combine with physical matter to create the Universe. . .
Be at one with the Universe. . . See yourself as a part of the WHOLE, one of many equal parts.
Be in the center of your head.
Come out of trance.
Bend over.

TWELFTH CHAKRA — ALL THAT IS

Location: Infinitely within and around you.
Function: TO BE.
Abilities: To be ALL THAT IS and ONE at the same time.
Disabilities: TO NOT BE.

#25 EXERCISE
Twelfth Chakra

Cosmic energy. . .pink gold

Earth energy. . .pink

Sit in your trance position.

Close your eyes.

Be in the center of your head.

Go into trance.

Ground yourself.

Run your energy.

The key to seeing and experiencing this Chakra is to be WHOLE—WORLD oriented. . . Without this intent, you will experience nothing. . .

Relax. . . Allow every cell in your Body to be grounded and relaxed. . .surrender yourself to the WHOLE. . . Allow every cell in your Body to be a part of all that is. . .all that was. . .all that ever will be. . .and BE. . . . . .

Be in the center of your head.

Come out of trance.

Bend over.

THE HUMAN AURA

Your *Aura* is a field of energy that emanates from and surrounds your Body. The Male-Female properties of the energy form patterns and colors which make a basic statement about you, your attitudes, moods, dispositions, thoughts and the happenings of your day. It is an autonomous expression of your individual self, reflecting who you are and drawing like energies to you that reaffirm that reflection. If you want to change another's attitude about you, simply change your attitude about yourself. The reflection of that attitude will draw to it validating energies.

Only *your* energy belongs in your Aura. This is your personal and private space. If reality were a house, your Aura would be your room. No one else lives in this space but you. No one else has a right to make decisions in or about this space but you. For some, their psychic opening is very much like cleaning house: becoming more aware of what needs fixing, cleaning, organizing or putting away. Welcome home!

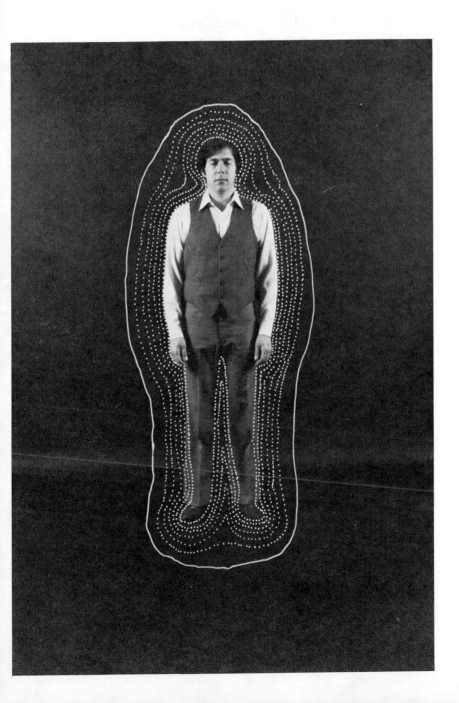

#26 EXERCISE
Human Aura

Cosmic energy. . .light orange
Earth energy. . .orange

Sit in your trance position.
Close your eyes.
Be in the center of your head.
Go into trance.
Ground yourself.
Run your energy.
Posulate that every cell in your Body, including every cell in your brain, gives off energy. . . Every cell in your Body reflects light and color. . .giving its own elemental expression of self. . . Feel this energy. . . Be the energy.
Be in the center of your head.
BE YOURSELF.
Come out of trance.
Bend over.

THE LAYERS OF YOUR AURA

A healthy Aura is in constant movement, changing from moment to moment. It is well defined with each of its seven layers maintaining themselves. The integrity of each layer is kept by the interaction of the electro-magnetic properties of the energy. Starting with the layer closest to your Body, they are as follows:

1...*Physical Body:*
> organs, bones, skin, muscle, blood, brain, cells, etc.; the health of your physical Body is shown by the vitality of the energy.

2...*Feelings:*
> about your Body, about your personality, about yourself, emotional balance and health.

3...*Thoughts and opinions:*
> about your Body, your personality, and yourself.

4...*Unprocessed feelings and thoughts:*
> about others, mental balance and health.

5...*Karma:*
> unfinished cycles.

6...*Belief systems:*
> attracting like Realities.

7...*Human Aura Boundaries:*
> openings, attraction, resistance.

#27 EXERCISE
Layers of the Aura

Cosmic energy. . .lavender
Earth energy. . .silver blue

Sit in your trance position.
Close your eyes.
Be in the center of your head.
Go into trance.
Ground yourself.
Run your energy.
Feel. . .see. . .experience your Aura: the energy
    . . .light. . .color around your Body. Notice
    the different layers. . . Notice the shapes of
    these layers. . . At what points of your Body
    do the layers pull in?. . . At what parts do the
    layers push out?. . . Where are they pushed
    together?. . . Where are they defined?. . .
    What colors do the layers have?. . . Where is
    there a lot of energy?. . . Where is there little
    energy?. . . How do the different layers feel?
    . . . How do they look?
BE YOURSELF. . .reaffirm that this is your
    space by saying *"my space, my Aura"* and
    allow those words to resonate from your Body
    to the edge of your Aura.
Be in the center of your head.
Come out of trance.
Bend over.

BOUNDARIES

Your *Boundaries* lie at the edge of the seventh layer of your Aura. It is where you end and the rest of the world begins. The walls of your Boundaries act as semi-permeable membranes to enable communication with another. To maintain your freedom and autonomy you must use your discretion when deciding which energies are yours and which are not; which problems are yours and which are not. When you start to work on another's problem (energy), you start to lose your Boundaries to that person. At that point you may begin to forget who you are and become that other person: their habits, styles, beliefs, emotions, thoughts and even their physical symptoms. Your freedom lies in knowing yourself: your problems, your thoughts, your judgments and opinions, likes and dislikes. When you know who you are, then you also know who you are not. Your Boundaries do not have to be thick and heavy for you to affirm yourself; it just needs to be well defined. An analogy would be a cell wall membrane.

#28 BOUNDARIES   Cosmic energy. . .sky blue
Boundaries   Earth energy. . .purple

Sit in your trance position.

Close your eyes.

Be in the center of your head.

Go into trance.

Ground yourself.

Run your energy.

From the center of your head, notice where your Boundaries are. . . Feel them about two feet from your Body. . . Now expand your Boundaries. . . Use your energy to fill up the room you are sitting in. . . Then expand your Aura to fill up the building that you are in. . .filling up every corner with your energy. Now fill up the city that you are in. . . Allow your energy to fill up the entire city. . .· Now fill up the State you are in. . . Notice that your energy and the energies of many others can be at the same place at the same time and NOT interfere with each other. . . Each energy moves at a different vibration. . . Now allow your energy to fill up the Country that you live in. . . Fill up the entire Country. . .expanding yourself. . .expanding your Boundaries (limits) . . . Expand your energy to the hemisphere that you are in. . .and to the Planet Earth. . .

Expand your energy to embrace the entire Planet Earth. . . Notice how the peoples on the Planet relate to each other. . . Feel the vibratory level of the Planet Earth. . . Now expand your Boundaries to the edges of the Universe. . . Fill up the Universe with your energy. . . Notice the edges of the Universe. . . Be aware of what part you play within this Universe. . . Be aware of:

ALL THAT IS everywhere... *omnipresent*

ALL THAT IS everything... *omnipotent*

ALL THAT IS all forms... *omnifarious*

ALL THAT IS all knowing... *omniscient*

ALL THAT IS ALL LOVING

Now gather yourself, your energy and pull yourself back into the Planet Earth. . .pulling your Boundaries into the shape and size of the Planet Earth. . . Pull your energy into the State. . .pulling in all your energy into that State. . . Next pull yourself back into the City . . . Pull your Boundaries into the shape and size of that City. . . Now pull your Boundaries and energy into the building. . .pulling back only yourself. . . Pull your Boundaries into the room. . .with your energy filling up the room . . .only your energy. . . Pull your Boundaries about two to three feet around your Body. . . taking up only as much space as you can be

responsible for. . .
BE YOURSELF.
Be in the center of your head.
Be in the present moment.
Come out of trance.
Bend over.

THE TWELVE LEVELS
OF CONSCIOUSNESS

As you become more conscious of yourself, you are becoming aware of the many levels of yourself. Each Chakra and each layer of your Aura has twelve levels of which to be conscious. This is your method of interaction, perception and organization of your energy.

INTERACTION: \ STATES:	STRUCTURAL	VIBRATIONAL	DIRECTIONAL	TRANSFOR–MATIONAL
INTRAPERSONAL	1. *Physical* reproductive physical Body	2. *Emotional* communicative biorhythm instincts feelings	3. *Causal* action movement	4. *Intuitive* understanding inner voice
INTERPERSONAL	5. *Psychological* personality patterns games styles relationships	6. *Psychic* energy patterns dreams imagination (unconscious activity)	7. *Analytical* thought processes	8. *Mathematical* geometric equations Astrology
TRANSPERSONAL	9. *Spiritual* Soul Oversoul	10. *Theoretical* a plan a probability	11. *Conceptual* an original idea a possibility	12. *God* the creative

#29 EXERCISE
Twelve Levels of
Consciousness

Cosmic energy. . .pink gold

Earth energy. . .white gold

Sit in your trance position.

Close your eyes.

Be in the center of your head.

Go into trance.

Ground yourself.

Run your energy.

Create a heart in front of you and let it represent that which you want to Know. . . Throw the question *Which Chakra do I use the most?* into the heart...When the heart disappears there will be a number...This first number is the Chakra...Then create another heart in front of you...Throw the question *What level of consciousness do I use most in that Chakra?*...When the heart disappears there will be a number...This is the level of consciousness.

Be up in the corner. . . Pull yourself up into the corner. . . From up in the corner look back at your Body, your Aura and Chakras. . . See the many levels where you can manifest yourself. . . See the multi-faceted ways of expressing that self. . . See it as your expression. . .within your control. . . You can be

anything that you want to be. . .
Be in the center of your head. . .
BE YOURSELF.
Come out of trance.
Bend over.

GENETIC KEY

The *Genetic Key* is the contract between you the Soul and you the Body. It is the meeting point where each of your multidimentional *I's* bond together to make agreements about what to do, how to manifest, what abilities to have, amount of potential and physical prowess and strength. Agreement or disagreement between Soul and Body will show up here.

The Genetic Key looks like a pronged fork. It contains the physical genetic predetermined qualities of energy that make up your Body, the genetic code. It fuses into your Body at your Heart Chakra. It comes in contact with you the Soul in the center of your head. The prongs of the fork plug into tiny sparks of energy just in front of the center of your head, somewhat like a control panel.

#30 EXERCISE
The Genetic Key

Cosmic energy. . .silver
Earth energy. . .copper

Sit in your trance position.

Close your eyes.

Be in the center of your head.

Go into trance.

Ground yourself.

Run your energy.

Go up in the corner and look down at your Body. . . Notice that the Genetic Key is at the left of your head. . . If it is not plugged into your Heart Chakra, then plug it in. . . Also plug the three top cords into the brain. . . Notice the color of your Genetic Key. . . If it is very dark, lighten it up. . . Keep it at its natural color. . .just lighten the tone of color . . . This will allow you to have your highest and fullest potential in your Body.

Pull yourself back into the center of your head.

Be in the center of your head.

Come out of trance.

Bend over.

PICTURES

As you experience your daily living, your mind takes reels and reels of mental film capturing your impressions of those experiences. If you were to stop that film and look at a single frame, you would be looking at a *picture.*

A picture has three basic components: the point, the charge and the chaff.

THE POINT is the POsitive INTent of the picture. What is the positive intention motivating you to receive or create the picture.

THE CHARGE in a picture represents the amount of emotion and/or trauma that you have attached to that experience.

THE CHAFF of a picture is the CHaracter AFFect. How is your character or personality, the way in which you take action affected by this picture. The affect is shown in both the action between your Selves (the Soul and the Body) and in the outer appearance of your action to the others.

The picture will have its own basic integrity, just as the situations in the experience did; and it will also be colored and formed by you as you process it, and integrate it into your energy Body.

The process starts first with your perception of the picture. You perceive and recognize the picture in one of your Seven Body Chakras.

7th Chakra: you *know* the energy that forms the picture.

6th Chakra: you *see* the energy that forms the picture.

5th Chakra: you *hear* the energy that forms the picture.

4th Chakra: you *become one* with the energy that forms the picture.

3rd Chakra: you *manipulate* the energy that forms the picture.

2nd Chakra: you *feel* the energy that forms the picture.

1st Chakra: you *ground through* the energy that forms the picture.

The picture travels through the Chakra into your Back Channels and into the center of your head. It is here that you analyze and discriminate the energy of the picture. If the energy is compatible with your energy, you will file it away in your memory banks. If the picture has a great deal of charge, it throws off electro-magnetic properties that act like the poles of a magnet. The picture will be cast out into the Aura or Chakras to be reprocessed later. The act of reprocessing can take place consciously as when you are meditating or talking out your problems, or subconsciously as in a dream state.

#31 EXERCISE
Picture

Cosmic energy. . .light green
Earth energy. . .forest green

Sit in your trance position.

Close your eyes.

Be in the center of your head.

Go into trance.

Ground yourself.

Run your energy.

From inside your memory banks, pull a picture of an ear of corn. . . Place it in front of your Sixth Chakra. . . Look at it. . . Pull it back into the center of your head, and file it back into your memory banks.

Go up in the corner and look back at your Body . . . Notice your Grounding Cord. . . Be aware of the difference of a mental image picture, such as one recalled from memory banks (the neutral image of the ear of corn), and a psychic image, such as the one you are experiencing when you look at your Grounding Cord.

Pull yourself back into your Body.

Be in the center of your Head.

Come out of trance.

Bend over.

Chapter Four

SELF-RESTRICTING ENERGY PATTERNS

STUCK PICTURE

FROZEN PICTURE

FROZEN ENERGY

ENERGY BLOCK

CRACK

SCREEN

SHIELD

MASK

HOLE

SYMBOL

MACHINE

BELIEF SYSTEMS

WORKING OFF OF
ANOTHER'S PICTURE

RUNNING A VALENCE

The following energy patterns act as prisons and uniforms that restrict you and keep you from being yourself. They stop the ebb and flow and balance of energy received and energy given because they are like a two-way prison: locking you in and the rest of the world out. The key to opening these prisons and taking off these uniforms is your determination to redirect your energy. Once you have taken full responsibility for your energy, you can change it at will.

Stuck Picture   Often the heavily charged pictures that are thrown into the Aura and Chakras for reprocessing are not reprocessed. They are avoided because they are experienced as a necessity for your survival or because of what the content makes you re-experience. This type of picture will gain enough charge to slow it down until it is stuck in one place in one particular time.

Stuck Energy   is energy that is caught on either side of a stuck picture.

Frozen Picture   is a picture that has gained enough charge from stuck energy that it has become frozen in one place and time within your energy system. Yet it is still somewhat transparent.

Frozen Energy   is energy that is stuck on either side of a frozen picture.

Energy Block   occurs when a collection of stuck pictures are attracting like energies and reaffirming pictures. With all these pictures validating each other, they become like a solid block of energy.

Crack	will appear when a block of energy is loosening its charge.
Screen	of energy is a network of pictures that acts as a filter screen. It allows certain energies to come in and keeps certain energies out. What you hold out you also hold in.
Shield	of energy is a network of pictures that holds out all energy. It also holds in all energy.
Mask	is energy shaped in a fixed expression you place between you and others.
Hole	is a lack of energy in one area caused by emptiness due to loss.
Symbol	in the Aura or Chakras represents achievements or desired memories from different times.
Machine	is like a slide projector, constantly projecting a picture or set of pictures automatically.

#32 EXERCISE
Self-Restricting
   Energy Patterns

Cosmic energy . . . yellow gold
Earth energy . . . lavender

Sit in your trance position.

Close your eyes.

Be in the center of your head.

Go into trance.

Ground yourself.

Run your energy.

Go up in the corner and look back down at your
    Body. . . What does the energy around your
    Body look like?. . . Is it in constant motion?
    . . .bright and active colors?. . . Are there
    frozen patches?. . .blocks?. . .shields?. . .
    holes?. . . Are there any machines projecting
    the same old energy patterns (the same old
    problems)?. . . Start to know yourself.

Pull yourself into the present moment.

Be in the center of your head.

Come out of trance.

Bend over.

BELIEF SYSTEMS

During the first five to seven years of your life you collect a certain amount of charged pictures that rule or govern the way you use your energy. You hold these pictures near the chakras they rule. If you were raised in a family where telepathy was not permitted, then you would have a set of pictures (beliefs) that would surround and deafen your clairaudient ears. You would continue to act on the belief that you cannot hear another's throughts, and that no one can hear your thoughts. Even if everyone around you was communicating telepathically, you would be unaware of it. If you were raised to believe that you are not worthy and therefore cannot have what you want in life, this system of pictures would set in your heart, and it would throw out any information contrary to the belief in your worth. Even if everyone you are around daily respects and appreciates your worth, you would not experience it because you would not believe it was true. You can create your experiences, both positive and negative, with your belief systems. When you change your beliefs, you ultimately change yourself and the reality you observe around you.

#33 EXERCISE
Belief Systems

Cosmic energy... pink
Earth energy. . .orange

Sit in your trance position.

Close your eyes.

Be in the center of your head.

Go into trance.

Ground yourself.

Run your energy.

Go up in the corner. . . Pull yourself up into the corner. . .and look back down at your Body . . . Notice where you hold your restricting belief systems. . . They will look like a set of pictures that are attached together. . .each singular picture not having that much charge . . .yet the collective charge from the number of pictures attached together keeps this energy formation from being filed in your memory banks. . .

Remember where these systems are, where you hold them. . . Now be in the center of your head. . . Pull one of your belief systems in front of you and look at it. . . Notice the limitations that system of pictures creates for you . . . Put it back. . . Now pull another belief system in front of you. . . Notice the limits this one holds for you. . . Put that belief back. . .

Remind yourself that you are NOT your beliefs.
Be in the center of your head.
Be the pure essence of yourself.
Come out of trance.
Bend over.

WORKING OFF OF
ANOTHER'S PICTURES

Working Off of Another's Pictures occurs any time you regard another's opinion, idea, thought, judgment or consideration before you regard your own. You are controlled by their energy.

#34 EXERCISE   Cosmic energy. . .light green
Working Off of   Earth energy. . .light yellow
Another's Pictures

Sit in your trance position.

Close your eyes.

Be in the center of your head.

Go into trance.

Ground yourself.

Run your energy.

Go up in the corner and look back down at your
Body. . . Allow all energies that are another's
pictures (opinions, ideas, thoughts, judgments
or considerations) to show up as dark areas. . .
Notice where you most often take these on. . .
Notice where you take another's energy as
more valid than your own. . .

Now be in the center of your head and in front
of you create the outline of a heart. . .and
throw all the energies that you saw as dark
into that heart. . . Allow that heart to have
wings so it will return all those energies to
their sources.

Be in the center of your head.

BE YOURSELF.

Come out of trance.

Bend over.

RUNNING A VALENCE

Whenever you decide that another does a certain act better than you, and you copy them as you do that act, you are running their *valence*. Every cell in your Body matches the energy of that person at the first time you decide to copy their actions. After awhile a valence becomes an automatic process. When that act needs to be performed, you recreate the picture of how that person works, and you put a cord into the past time when you first decided to run your energy this way. At that moment you have matched energy that is at a fixed point in time.

#35 EXERCISE
Releasing a Valence

Cosmic energy. . .lavender
Earth energy. . .rose pink

Sit in your trance position.

Close your eyes.

Be in the center of your head.

Go into trance.

Ground yourself.

Run your energy.

Choose a single valence to work on.

Postulate that you have a picture of this person in every cell in your Body. . . Postulate that you are connecting every picture from every cell in your Body. . .

In the center of the room place a large outline of a heart, and from the crown of your head start to throw off and out of your Body these reels and reels of pictures. . . Start at the top of your head. . .running this film off of every cell in your head. . .into the heart in the center of the room. . .off of every facial muscle. . .off of your eyes, your Sixth Chakra . . .your mouth. . .your Fifth Chakra. . .the back of your head. . . Let go of all the thoughts of that picture. . . Run the film off of your shoulders and your arms. . .into the center of the room. . .off your hands. . . Let go of every movement that is connected to that picture. . . Let go of the pictures from your chest, your Heart Chakra. . .off of your back. . .out of your spine. . . Run that film off and out of your Third Chakra. . .out into the center of the room. . .your lower back. . . Allow every cell to let go of this picture. . . your Second Chakra. . . Let go of all emotions having to do with that picture. . . Allow the film to flow into the center of the room from your pelvic cradle. . .your genitals . . .your buttocks. . .your First Chakra. . . Allow all the film in your legs to run into the center of the room. . .and finally from your feet. . . Let go of every memory of that valence from every cell in your Body. . . . . .

Allow the heart to have wings, and send all that energy back to the person you have matched. Bring your attention point (cord) away from this past experience and into the present moment.

Be in the center of your head.

BE YOURSELF.

Be in the present moment.

Come out of trance.

Bend over.

PLEASE NOTE:

You may need to do this exercise several times before it takes effect.

Chapter Five

CREATE YOUR OWN REALITY

TAKING RESPONSIBILITY FOR
YOURSELF

SELF-REALIZATION

CLEARING

SELF HEALING

DEVELOPING YOUR
PSYCHIC ABILITIES

CREATING YOUR
PERSONAL UNIVERSE

CREATE YOUR OWN REALITY

The energy around you attracts like energies to you. In this way, by your thoughts, feelings and actions you directly or indirectly create your own reality. When you create your reality indirectly, it seemingly appears created for you, with you as the victim carried along by fate. To directly create your own reality you must first take full responsibility for yourself. This means that you respond fully to all your abilities: the ability to survive, to feel, to be powerful, to be in affinity with yourself and others, to communicate, to see and know your energy. The next step would be to recognize and discriminate whether the energy is your's or another's. The third step in this process would be the act of the creation of your own energy Universe.

The following techniques and exercises will give you an opportunity to discover yourself, clear yourself, heal yourself, develop yourself and create your personal reality to your liking. Allow yourself to change and grow.

TAKING RESPONSIBILITY FOR YOURSELF

When you are using the process of psychic self-development you need to have a few tools or techniques to help you in recognizing and taking responsibility for yourself. It is the acceptance of this responsibility which allows you to take control of your energy.

How To See Your Essence Energy

The only truth in your Aura and Chakras is you, your own pure essence energy. It is energy that comes from the very depths of your Soul. All other energies are a lie state to you. Once you have an idea of who you are on an energy level, you can start to weed out who you are not, ridding yourself of energy patterns and levels that are not yours.

#36 EXERCISE
Discovering Your
Essence Energy

Cosmic energy. . .pink gold
Earth energy. . .pink gold

Sit in your trance position.

Close your eyes.

Be in the center of your head.

Go into trance.

Ground yourself.

Run your energy.

Imagine, if you will, that you are wrapped in a
cocoon. . . You, on a Soul level, are covered
with threads of energy that are not you. . .
threads of energy that make up your Body. . .
. . . threads of energy that are others' ideas
. . . threads of energy that are others' ideads
and realities. . . All these threads become a
cocoon of energy that is hiding the pure
essence within it. . . the core of your Being. . .

Allow these threads of energy to fly off of you
. . . They will fly off in all directions. . . All
of the threads fly off, and you can start to feel
who you are. . . As the rest of the threads fly
off you can feel your freedom. This is your
true essence. . . Feel your freedom. Feel your
autonomy. . . . Feel your wings spread open
as if you were a butterfly. . . This is who you
are on an energy level. . . BE this energy

. . . Notice the temperature, the movement,
the weight, viscosity, texture, shape, tone and
color of the energy. . . Know yourself on an
energy level. . . BE YOURSELF.

Be in the center of your head.

Come out of trance.

Bend over.

HOW TO TELL THE TRUTH FROM A LIE

The *truth* is a function not only of the physical event or action itself, but also of the attendant emotions, words, thoughts, images, pictures, desires, and beliefs. The truth is a natural energy consequence of the events and components that support it. It is singular by nature. You can find the truth by looking at any one of its components because every part supports and is in agreement with the other parts giving you the feeling of one WHOLE; there are no deviations on any level for you to consider.

A *lie*, in comparison, is a natural consequence when the information (emotions, words, thoughts, images, pictures, desires, and beliefs) does not support the physical event or action. Each of its components says something different. Because of this complexity, it has to be remembered by the one lying. The burden is the lie itself and the prison is all the contradictory information that is needed to defend it or cover it up. To a clairvoyant a lie looks like an X in the Aura or Chakras: the picture of the lie superimposed on the picture of the truth. Because it takes a large amount of energy to maintain this set of pictures, the one lying may appear to be somewhat unconscious or scattered, with not enough energy to manifest themselves completely in the Physical Reality.

#37 EXERCISE
Lies

Cosmic energy...pink
Earth energy...rose pink

Sit in your trance position.

Close your eyes.

Be in the center of your head.

Go into trance.

Ground yourself.

Run your energy.

Go up in the corner...and look back at your Body and the Aura around your Body...Do you see any lies?...If so, where?...

Be in the center of your head...and take that lie you saw, and place it in front of you...Pull the pictures apart and look at both pictures: the lie...the truth...Evaluate the differences and why you chose the lie...Forgive yourself.

Blow up and release the energy connected with the lie. Neutralize that energy...Collect the energy of the truth that is in front of you. Pull both the neutralized energy and the truth into your Crown Chakra and all the way into your Body...

Be your own truth.

BE YOURSELF.

Be in the center of your head.

Come out of trance.

Bend over.

How To Release a Picture

Besides any of the preceding energy patterns that you may carry around in your Aura and Chakras, you are also surrounded by your daily thoughts: ideas, plans, emotions, experiences and neutral pictures. You are a great creator. There can be a problem if you have an attachment to these creations and keep them in your Aura because they start collecting other energies. When you find yourself burdened by your thoughts and daily experiences, you must release or let go of the pictures involved.

#38 EXERCISE
Releasing a Picture

Cosmic energy. . .violet
Earth energy. . .violet

Sit in your trance position.
Close your eyes.
Be in the center of your head.
Go into trance.
Ground yourself.
Run your energy.
From the center of your head pick an idea that
   you have flying around in your Aura. . .an
   idea that you had today. . .one that has reoc-
   curred a few times. . .a neutral idea, one
   without charge. . .
Take the idea (picture) and place it in front of
   your Sixth Chakra. . . Notice the picture and
   hold it in front of you (this can be done within your Aura). . . Take a little of your own
   pure essence energy. . .neutral essence energy
   . . .and throw it at the picture. . . The picture
   will dissolve. . . The energy will be neutralized. . .and you will let go of the picture.
Be in the center of your head.
Come out of trance.
Bend over.

How to Release a Charged Picture

Some of your daily energy pictures will have too much charge to be gently released. Because of the intensity of their charge, these pictures need a little more energy from you to be released. You must actually blow up the heavily charged picture: break the formation of its energy into pieces to dissolve it and let go of it. You are dealing with *your* mental image pictures. Therefore, no harm will come to those whose images you blow up. It is *your energy* that you are releasing.

#39 EXERCISE
Releasing a
Charged Picture

Cosmic energy. . .sky blue
Earth energy. . .light green

Sit in your trance position.
Close your eyes.
Be in the center of your head.
Go into trance.
Ground yourself.
Run your energy.
Pick a picture from your Aura that is upsetting
to you. . .having to do with your mother. . .
Place that picture in front of your Aura,
beyond your Boundaries. . .outside your Aura
. . . Now zap it with your energy (use the
emotionally charged energy that holds you to
that picture. . . Are you angry, jealous, hurt?)
. . . As the picture blows up, it is neutralized
. . . You will file the neutralized picture into
your memory banks.
Be in the center of your head.
Forgive yourself for having charged pictures.
Love yourself for taking control of your energy.
Come out of trance.
Bend over.

How To Clean Yourself Out

Your personal freedom lies within the unlimited expression of your energy. If you are clogged up with stuck pictures, other people's energy, today's thoughts, any energy formation, sooner or later your energy will be limited. You will be limited, not able to show and be yourself. Any energy pattern that alters the pure intent of your energy is destructive to your freedom. Cleaning out your Aura, Chakras, energy Channels and circuitry on a daily level is important in maintaining your freedom.

#40 EXERCISE   Earth energy. . .pink gold
How To Clean Yourself Out

Sit in your trance position.

Close your eyes.

Be in the center of your head.

Go into trance.

Ground yourself.

Open up your Feet Chakras and pull into them a pure, pink gold Earth energy. . . Allow this energy to wash through your leg Channels. . . pushing out all blocks and pictures. . . Allow this energy to wash through your legs and down your Grounding Cord and then into your spine, cleaning out your Grounding Cord and your back Channels. . .pushing up and out all self-created and other-created energy patterns that are not in this present moment with you. . . Allow this energy to wash directly up through your legs and up your back Channels. . .and out the crown of your head . . .letting go of all energies not in this present moment.

As this pink gold Earth energy is washing through your Channels, allow it to wash out each of your Body Chakras. . .starting at the base of your spine with your First Chakra. . . to the Seventh Chakra. . .and your hand

Chakras. . .letting go of all attachments to
any energy. . .giving yourself a psychic bath.
Now take the energy from within your Channels
and expand it. . . As it expands, it is pushing
all the energy wastes to the outside edge of
your Aura. . . The pink gold Earth energy is
flushing up and out all unwanted energy
patterns. . .sending energy that belongs to
others back to them. . .cleaning and neutralizing your pictures. . .allowing your pure
essence energy to manifest. . .
BE YOURSELF.
Be in the center of your head.
Come out of trance.
Bend over.

How To Rid Your Body
of Excess Nervous Energy

At times you will find yourself feeling very nervous. This is due to too much energy in your Chakras. It may be one or all the Chakras. Even if it is only one Chakra that is over energized, drain all of them. You will only drain off the excess, and no more. You will not be weakened, you will be balanced. This exercise is excellent for insomniacs. For that purpose, lay down in your bed.

#41 EXERCISE
How To Rid Your Body of Excess Nervous Energy

Sit in your trance position.

Close your eyes.

Be in the center of your head.

Go into trance.

Ground yourself.

Take all the excess energy in your First Chakra and send it down your Grounding Cord. . . Then take all the excess energy from your Second Chakra and dump it down your Grounding Cord. . . Then the nervous energy . . .excess energy in your Third Chakra. . . dump all of that energy in your Grounding Cord. . .ground out all that energy.

The excess nervous energy from your upper four Body Chakras will go up your back Channels and out the crown of your head. . . This psychically charged energy may appear as lightning bolts arching off of your Crown Chakra. . . Drain off your Fourth Chakra. . . allowing all the excess energy to go up your Channels and arch off the top of your head . . . The your Fifth Chakra. . .let go of the excess energy. . .and your Sixth Chakra. . . Let go of all those nervous thoughts. . .allow

the thoughts as energy to drain up and out. . .
then your Seventh Chakra. . .let go of your
nervous energy. . . Allow all the nervous
energy to either go down your Grounding
Cord or out the top of your head.

Be in the center of your head.

Come out of trance.

Bend over.

To Get an Answer: Ask a Question

The secret to finding your own answers simply lies within asking your own questions. Trust yourself to find the answer and accept what you get. If you feel blocked, clean yourself out with Earth energy, and ask again.

#42 EXERCISE   Cosmic energy. . .light orange
Finding Your   Earth energy. . .light yellow
   Own Answers

Sit in your trance position.
Close your eyes.
Be in the center of your head.
Go into trance.
Ground yourself.
Run your energy.
Place an outline of a heart in front of you. . .
   Let it represent what you want to know. . .
   Take a question such as *"What will be my next level of growth?"* and throw it into the heart. . . As the two energies meet, the answer will appear. . .
Be in the center of your head.
Come out of trance.
Bend over.

Seniority

Because all the levels of YOU are made up of
your energy, you hold a certain status over your
space. No one else has created your space, and
unless you say so, no one has a right to take your
space. You are *senior* in your space. Your acknowl-
edgment and reaffirming beliefs of this will make
it so.

#43 EXERCISE
Seniority

Cosmic energy. . .sky blue

Earth energy. . .pink

Sit in your trance position.

Close your eyes.

Be in the center of your head.

Go into trance.

Ground yourself.

Run your energy.

Choose someone who intimidates you. . .someone of whom you are afraid. . . Place an image of then in the center of the room. . . As if you were playing a game of tag, leave your Body and go out in the center of the room and tag this person on the shoulder. . . Then run back into your Body. . . Notice that the other does not come into your Aura, and because you are running at a different vibration, even if they try, you are like a cloud to them. . . Feel the power and safety of your own personal energy.

Be in the center of your head.

Come out of trance.

Bend over.

How To Feel Confident

When you are in an uncomfortable situation: in a crowd, meeting new people, interviewing for a job, at a party, performing on stage, etc., and you want to feel at ease, relaxed, confident and on top of things. . .all you need is a solid Grounding Cord. You need to *own the room.*

#44 EXERCISE
Own the Room

This exercise is to be done out of trance. . .or in
a very light, eyes-open trance. . .

Wherever you are, with your eyes open, be in
the center of your head and ground yourself
. . . Make a strong connection to the Planet
. . . After you are grounded. . .send out eight
energy cords and grab all eight corners of the
room. . . Send two from each foot to the four
floor corners and four from your crown to the
ceiling corners. . . As you grab these corners,
say to yourself *"my Room"*. . . You will notice
that with your energy vibrating at your own
frequency and everyone else's energy vibrating
at their own frequencies, that everyone in the
room can own the room at the same time and
still allow for the others to do so at the same
time. . . The more you practice this, the
easier it will be to do under stress. . .

How To Protect Yourself

Your greatest protection is really a nonprotection: simply to KNOW YOURSELF. When you know who you are on an energy level, then you know who you are not! When another sends you an opinion or judgment, you will recognize that the energy is not yours and therefore does not belong in your Aura. With an open Grounding Cord all other energies will be continuously flushed down your Grounding Cord into the center of the Earth and eventually back to them. If you have pictures of which you are not aware, or shields and blocks, and another sends you an opinion or a judgment, then their picture will get stuck on your picture and be unable to go down your Grounding Cord. At that point in your Aura there will be an overcharged area. You will notice this as a painful experience, for another's energy does not belong in your space. If it stays there long enough, you will start to believe that it is true. If you do not know who you are, then you will believe the lies of others, or your own lies. As you can see, the more aware you are of yourself, the safer you are.

SELF—REALIZATION

Now that you have some tools to take control of your own energy, you will use those tools to discover and realize who you are. When you start to get your information, use your three period pause [. . .] to reflect on it.

The following exercises are designed to help you discover yourself; to realize who you are as separate from what you think or feel and to realize how you react in any given situation. These exercises will give you a greater understanding of yourself.

#45 EXERCISE
First Hello

Cosmic energy. . .lavender
Earth energy. . .sky blue

Sit in your trance position.

Close your eyes.

Be in the center of your head.

Go into trance.

Ground yourself.

Run your energy.

As if you were on a railroad track and this track were a time track. . .the lights that you see are the charged past pictures. . .this time you will go back in time on the track until a strong bright light appears. . . Go back to the first time you ever said hello to someone. . . Who was it?. . . How was it given?. . . How was it received?

Next to back on your time track to the first time anyone else said hello to you. . . What did they mean?. . . What did they want?. . . How was it given and how did you receive it?

Be in present time.

Be yourself.

Come out of trance.

Bend over.

#46 EXERCISE   Cosmic energy. . .light yellow
First Body,   Earth energy. . .light green
  Original Purpose

Sit in your trance position.

Close your eyes.

Be in the center of your head.

Go into trance.

Ground yourself.

Run your energy.

As if you were on a railroad track, go back in time to the first time you took a Body on this Planet. . . How long ago was it?. . . What was your purpose for coming here?. . . Who are you?. . .

Be in the center of your head.

BE YOURSELF.

Come out of trance.

Bend over.

#47 EXERCISE
Gathering Up
Your Energy

Cosmic energy. . .sky blue
Earth energy. . .pink

Sit in your trance position.
Close your eyes.
Be in the center of your head.
Go into trance.
Ground yourself.
Run your energy.
Postulate that all the energy that you have given away is coming back to you in the form of bright golden dots of energy. . . Since no one else can use your energy, you can bring it all back without hurting or denying anyone.
Be in the center of your head.
Have all of your potential.
Come out of trance.
Bend over.

#48 EXERCISE   Cosmic energy. . .sky blue
Releasing Another's   Earth energy. . .light green
  Energy

Sit in your trance position.

Close your eyes.

Be in the center of your head.

Go into trance.

Ground yourself.

Run your energy.

Go up in the corner... Notice your Body... Allow all the energy that belongs to others to light up brown... Send it all back to them... Another's energy will only be stuck in your Aura... There is nothing good in it for you or the other by keeping their energy... Send it all back... You do not have to see and know whose energy it is... just postualate that it will go where it belongs... There is a certain power within the commanding nature of your postulations.

Create a bright, golden ball of energy and pull it into the crown of your head. . . Allow this energy to fill up any holes or gaps caused by releasing the other's energy.

Be in the center of your head.

Bring every cell in your Body into the present moment.

Be yourself.
Come out of trance.
Bend over.

#49 EXERCISE
First Viewpoint

Cosmic energy. . .purple
Earth energy. . .silver blue

Sit in your trance position.

Close your eyes.

Be in the center of your head.

Go into trance.

Ground yourself.

Run your energy.

On your time track. . .go back to the first time you looked at someone. . . What was your viewpoint?

Be in Present time.

Be in the center of your head.

Be yourself.

Come out of trance.

Bend over.

#50 EXERCISE
First Unconscious

Cosmic energy. . .silver blue
Earth energy. . .sky blue

Sit in your trance position.

Close your eyes.

Be in the center of your head.

Go into trance.

Ground yourself.

Run your energy.

On your time track. . .go back in time to the first time you were made unconscious by another (either by an insult or mild hypnotism). . . Notice how programmable you are when you are unconscious. . .

Be in Present time.

Be in the center of your head.

BE YOURSELF.

Come out of trance.

Bend over.

#51 EXERCISE
Invalidation

Cosmic energy. . .silver blue
Earth energy. . .sky blue

Sit in your trance position.

Close your eyes.

Be in the center of your head.

Go into trance.

Ground yourself.

Run your energy.

Create a heart in front of you. . . Choose three people who have invalidated you in the past and place them in this heart. . . Choose three people in the present who have invalidated you and place them in the heart. . . Choose three people in the future who may invalidate you and place them in the heart. . . Blow up the heart and release the energy. . . Forgive yourself for being invalidated. . .and give yourself permission to be right without validation from others. . . Change the released energy into certainty and bring it into your Crown Chakra and all the way into your Body.

Be in the center of your head.

Be in present time.

Come out of trance.

Bend over.

#52 EXERCISE
First Anger

Cosmic energy. . .sky blue
Earth energy. . .lavender

Sit in your trance position.

Close your eyes.

Be in the center of your head.

Go into trance.

Ground yourself.

Run your energy.

On your time track, go back to the first time
   you every got angry at someone. . . How was
   it received?. . . What decision did you make
   about your anger at that moment?. . . Give
   yourself permission to get angry. . .

Be in the center of your head.

Be in the present time.

Come out of trance.

Bend over.

#53 EXERCISE   Cosmic energy. . .light orange
Criticism   Earth energy. . .rose pink

Sit in your trance position.
Close your eyes.
Be in the center of your head.
Go into trance.
Ground yourself.
Run your energy.
On your time track, to back to the first time
     you were ever criticized. . . How was it given
     to you?. . . How did you take it?. . . What
     decision did you make at that time about
     criticism?
Be in the center of your head.
Be in present time.
Come out of trance.
Bend over.

#54 EXERCISE   Cos. energy. . .ultra light violet
First Show of Power   Earth energy. . .silver

Sit in your trance position.
Close your eyes.
Be in the center of your head.
Go into trance.
Ground yourself.
Run your energy.
On your time track, go back to the first time
    you ever showed your power to someone. . .
    How did you show it?. . . How was it re-
    ceived?. . . What decision did you make about
    your power?
Be in the center of your head.
Bring every cell in your Body into present time.
Come out of trance.
Bend over.

#55 EXERCISE
Recognition of
Male or Female

Cosmic energy. . .sky blue
Earth energy. . .pink

Sit in your trance position.
Close your eyes.
Be in the center of your head.
Go into trance.
Ground yourself.
Run your energy.
On your time track. . .go back to the first person
   who recognized what sex you were as you
   were born. . . What was their feeling about
   you as a male or female?. . . What did they
   expect of you?. . .
Be in this present moment. . . Come back to
   present time.
Be in the center of your head.
BE YOURSELF.
Come out of trance.
Bend over.

#56 EXERCISE
Seeking and Giving Recognition

Cosmic energy. . .sky blue
Earth energy. . .copper

Sit in your trance position.

Close your eyes.

Be in the center of your head.

Go into trance.

Ground yourself.

Run your energy.

Recall the kind of recognition that you received as a child. . . Do you believe that your parents gave you enough?. . . Was it positive or negative?. . . How did your parents compliment you?. . . How did they criticize you? . . . What words were used?. . . What non-verbal messages of recognition were used. . . dirty looks?. . . Consider your current recognition patterns. . . Do you now copy the recognition patterns your parents used with you?. . . What patterns have you successfully changed?. . . Is there anyone in your life now in present time giving you the same kind of recognition as your parents did?. . .

Be in the center of your head.

Forgive yourself for any energy patterns that you do not like in yourself.

Be in present time.

Come out of trance.

Bend over.

#57 EXERCISE
First I Love You

Cosmic energy. . .lavender
Earth energy. . .light purple

Sit in your trance position.

Close your eyes.

Be in the center of your head.

Go into trance.

Ground yourself.

Run your energy.

On your time track, go back to the first time someone ever said *"I love you"* to you. . . How was it meant?. . . What did that person expect in return?. . . How did you receive it?

Go back to the first time you said *"I love you"* to someone. . . How was it received?. . . What decision did you make about love at that time?. . . What decision can you make in present time with this past information?

Blow up all the pictures that restrict you from being in present time with your ability to love and be loved. Change the released energy into neutral energy and bring it in the Crown of your head.

Bring every cell of your body into the present moment.

Be in the center of your head.

Come out of trance.

Bend over.

#58 EXERCISE   Cosmic energy. . .pink gold
Havingness (What You   Earth energy. . .pink
Allow Yourself To Have)

Sit in your trance position.
Close your eyes.
Be in the center of your head.
Go into trance.
Ground yourself.
Run your energy.
Go up in the corner. . . Look back at your Heart
    Chakra. . . Ask your Heart Chakra how much
    you are allowed to *have*. . . Ask for a percent-
    age out of a whole of 100% . . . Look at the
    picture that is keeping you from having all of
    what you need and want. . . Blow the picture
    up. . . Pick three people in your past who
    would not let you *have*. . . Pick three people
    in your present who will not let you *have*. . .
    Pick three people in the future who may not
    let you *have*. . . Place these people in a heart
    and blow them up.
Change the released energy into your highest
    level of creativity. . .
Bring this energy into your Crown Chakra and
    fill yourself up with this high level of crea-
    tivity.
Be in present time.

Be in the center of your head.
Come out of trance.
Bend over.

#59 EXERCISE
Play, Fun

Cosmic energy. . .turquoise
Earth energy. . .turquoise

Sit in your trance position.

Close your eyes.

Be in the center of your head.

Go into trance.

Ground yourself.

Run your energy.

See yourself as a child at play. . . What did your parents say about your play?. . . What non-verbal messages were you given?. . . Were you given time to play autonomously, or was your play always structured?. . . Did you play alone?. . .with a friend?. . .an imaginary friend?. . . What were your active forms of play?. . . Where did you play?. . . Which was your favorite place and why?. . . What roles did you play?. . . Were you a follower or a leader?. . . What made you laugh?. . . Were you funny?. . . Did anyone tell you not to laugh?. . . Did anyone laugh at you?. . . Is play a part of your life now??????????

Be in the center of your head.

Enjoy yourself!

Come out of trance.

Bend over.

#60 EXERCISE
Work Space,
Home Space

Cosmic energy. . .light orange

Earth energy. . .light orange

Sit in your trance position.

Close your eyes.

Be in the center of your head.

Go into trance.

Ground yourself.

Run your energy.

Go up in the corner and look back down at your Body. . . When you throw the question, "*Where is my work space?*" at your Body, what Chakra lights up? This is the Chakra center where you go to figure out your problems and find your solutions. . .

Throw the question, "*Where is my home space?*" . . . What Chakra lights up as the question touches it? This is where you go when you want to be at home. . .and comfortable. . .to feel safe.

If you want to change your work space or home space. . ., simply place your attention on another Chakra when you need to go to work or home. . .

Be in the center of your head.

Come out of trance.

Bend over.

CLEARING

These exercises will help you release any charge you have within certain pictures and clear out programming so you can be who you are and clear out who you are not.

This is a reminder that when you release a picture, or even blow up a picture, you are working with your own energy and you are not harming in any way those you have blown up. If their energy is locked up with yours, then you are doing both of you a favor by releasing it. Use either the releasing technique or the blowing-up technique. Allow yourself to take control of your own energy.

#61 EXERCISE
Mother or Father

Cosmic energy. . .sky blue
Earth energy. . .green

Sit in your trance position.

Close your eyes.

Be in the center of your head.

Go into trance.

Ground yourself.

Run your energy.

Pull from your Aura a picture of your Mother (or Father). . .of her (his) judging you in some way. . . Feel the intensity of the energy. . . Notice the colors. . . Notice how you react to that picture. . . Neutralize the picture by blowing it up. . .

Place an outline of a heart in front of you. . . Place the neutral energy inside the heart. . . also place in the heart permission for you to have your own opinions about yourself. . . Pull this heart into your Heart Chakra and into your energy system. . .filling up any holes in your Aura with permission. . .

Be in the center of your head.

BE YOURSELF.

Come out of trance.

Bend over.

#62 EXERCISE
Survival Pictures

Cosmic energy. . .turquoise
Earth energy. . .yellow

Sit in your trance position.

Close your eyes.

Be in the center of your head.

Go into trance.

Ground yourself.

Run your energy.

Look at your First Chakra and notice if there is any energy that does not belong there. . . Allow it to show up as dark patches. . . This will be the opinions of others about your style of surviving. . . In front of your Auric Boundaries place a heart with wings. . . Throw into that heart all the pictures and energy that are not yours. . .all the opinions that you usually consider. . .all the judgments that bring you down. . . Throw all these pictures into the heart in front of you. . . Take the charge that you have and throw it at the heart in front of you. . . Neutralize the energy. . . Allow any energy that is not yours to go back to whomever it belongs and pull your neutralized energy back into your Aura. . .to fill up any areas just cleaned out with neutralized energy . . .for you to use as you manifest yourself.

Be in the center of your head.
BE YOURSELF.
Come out of trance.
Bend over.

#63 EXERCISE
Changing a Style of Survival

Cosmic energy. . .yellow
Earth energy. . .light green

Sit in your trance position.
Close your eyes.
Be in the center of your head.
Go into trance.
Ground yourself.
Run your energy.
Create a large heart in front of you. . . Choose something from your style of surviving that you want to change. . . From every cell in your Body throw off the energy that has to do with that style. . . Throw any pictures from Your Aura and Chakras having to do with that style. . .and blow it up. . .neutralizing the energy. . . With the neutral energy create in front of you exactly what style of surviving you will replace the other with. . . When you get a clear idea pull it into your Body. . . Absorb the information in every cell in your Body.
Be in the center of your head.
Come out of trance.
Bend over.

#64 EXERCISE

Cosmic energy. . .silver blue

Earth energy. . .violet

Certainty

(Sure of Yourself)

Sit in your trance position.

Close your eyes.

Be in the center of your head.

Go into trance.

Ground yourself.

Run your energy.

Pick three people from present time to whom you have given your certainty. . . Pick three people in past time to whom you gave your certainty. . .and pull your certainty back from the past and from the present. . . Be sure of yourself. . . Certainty is believing in yourself. . . Blow up all these images. . .recycle the energy. . .send theirs back to them and yours to you. . .

Be in the center of your head.

Come out of trance.

Bend over.

#65 EXERCISE
Picture Blowing

Cosmic energy...sky blue
Earth energy...green

Sit in your trance position.

Close your eyes.

Be in the center of your head.

Go into trance.

Ground yourself.

Run your energy.

Any time that you feel stuck on a picture, you can place the picture in front of you. . . pictures of your mother, your father, a teacher, a picture of your inability to manifest. . .any picture that has your energy stuck . . . Place that picture in a heart in front of you and throw your charge at it to neutralize it. . . Be sure to return the neutralized energy to your Aura, and fill up any openings created by the picture blowing.

Be in the center of your head.

BE YOURSELF.

Come out of trance.

Bend over.

#66 EXERCISE
Emotions and
Validation

Cosmic energy. . .light green
Earth energy. . .light orange

Sit in your trance position.

Close your eyes.

Be in the center of your head.

Go into trance.

Ground yourself.

Run your energy.

Pick three people in present time who want you to feel their emotions. . .who can only be validated in this way. . . Place a heart in front of you and place these three people in the heart. . .and blow them up.

Pick three people from your past who have wanted you to validate their emotions by feeling them. . . Throw these pictures into a heart in front of you and blow it up. . .

Pick three people who in the future might seek validation from you in this manner. Place them in a heart in front of you and blow them up. . . Release the hold that they have on you.

Gather all the neutralized energy and pull it into the Crown of your head. . . Pull it into the holes and gaps created by the clearing process.

Be in the center of your head.

Have your own emotions.
Come out of trance.
Bend over.

#67 EXERCISE
Power

Cosmic energy. . .yellow gold

Earth energy. . .pink gold

Sit in your trance position.

Close your eyes.

Be in the center of your head.

Go into trance.

Ground yourself.

Run your energy.

On your time track. . .go back to the first time that you felt powerless. . . To whom did you give your power?. . . For what reason?. . . Blow up the picture and pull your power back . . . Take all of your power back and pull yourself into present time.

Be in the center of your head.

Be powerful.

Come out of trance.

Bend over.

#68 EXERCISE   Cosmic energy. . .white gold
Unworthy Pictures   Earth energy. . .light violet

Sit in your trance position.

Close your eyes.

Be in the center of your head.

Go into trance.

Ground yourself.

Run your energy.

Look at your Heart Chakra, around it and in front of it. . . Are there any energy formations, pictures that appear dark or heavy, gloomy?. . . These patterns of energy will attract like energies giving you a double message of unworthiness, a kind of double jeopardy: first by the pictures themselves, and secondly by the reaffirming experiences that were drawn to those pictures.

Be in the center of your Heart. . . Notice that you see everything filtered by those pictures . . . Be in the center of your Head. . . Place a heart in front of you and let all the *I am not worthy* pictures from within and around the Heart Chakra go into that heart in front of you. . .throwing all the energy that has to do with those pictures into that heart in front of you. . . Take the amount of charge that you feel for those pictures, and throw it at the heart. . .blowing up all the pictures and neutralizing the energy. . . Change that heart full of neutralized energy into energy that would represent your highest level of worth and pull that heart into the Crown of your head. . . Pull it all the way into your Body.

Be in the center of your head.

Come out of trance.

Bend over.

#69 EXERCISE
Name

Cosmic energy. . .turquoise
Earth energy. . .pink

Sit in your trance position.

Close your eyes.

Be in the center of your head.

Go into trance.

Ground yourself.

Run your energy.

To find the answer to your questions, create a heart in front of you. . . Throw your question at the heart, and as they meet, your answer will form. . .

Who named you?. . . Why?. . . Who were you named after?. . . Did the name hold some expectations?. . . Was your name so popular that you felt like part of a mob?. . .or so uncommon that you felt odd?. . . If you have a nickname, where did you get it?. . . Do you like your name?. . . If not, would you like another name?. . . If so. . .throw that desire into a heart in front of you. . . What is the name that appears?

Be in the center of your head.

BE YOURSELF.

Come out of trance.

Bend over.

#70 EXERCISE   Cosmic energy. . .rose pink
Guilt   Earth energy. . .pink

Sit in your trance position.

Close your eyes.

Be in the center of your head.

Go into trance.

Ground yourself.

Run your energy.

Allow yourself to recall the most recent situation
in which you felt guilty. . . Guilt is a form of
punishing yourself. . . From a neutral space,
look at the situation, forgive yourself and see
if the guilt was yours. . .or did someone else
lay that guilt energy on you. . . Who in that
situation resents you. . . Resentment is a
demand that the other feel guilty. . .(resentment is used by someone who believes themselves to be a victim. . .the one they resent
becomes the oppressor). . . It is not your
energy; therefore, it is not your problem: let
go of the guilt. . . Blow up a picture of the
person who wanted you to take the blame
with guilt as your punishment. . .

On your time track, go back in time to the first
time you felt guilty. . . Notice the situation. . .
Were you wrong?. . . Who wanted you to
feel guilty and why?. . .(some parents feel

powerless around their children so they use guilt to discipline). . . See this original guilt with your adult eye...Be in present time... Blow up a picture of the person who originally wanted you to be the wrong one. . .the person who gave you the picture (idea) that you should be guilty. . .

Take all the neutralized energy in front of you and gather it up into a large golden sun... Pull this sun into your Crown Chakra and down into your Body. . .filling up any gaps or holes made by clearing the picture.

Be in the center of your head.

Be in present time.

Come out of trance.

Bend over.

#71 **EXERCISE**   Cosmic energy. . .light green
Fear   Earth energy. . .lavender

Sit in your trance position.

Close your eyes.

Be in the center of your head.

Go into trance.

Ground yourself.

Pick one person from present time of whom you are afraid. . . Place their image in front of you. . . Enlarge that image so that it is bigger than you. . . Now shrink that image so that it is smaller than you. . . On an energy level, fear is a misconceived survival mechanism. . . *If I become really small, they won't see me; I can hide.* . .so you pull your Boundaries in and condense all your energy into one small space. . . This is how fear gives you an overload of sorts that becomes super sensitive.

Push your Boundaries out to about three feet around you and fill up your Aura with your energy. . . Own your space. . . Now how do you feel about the person of whom you are afraid?. . . Blow up the picture. . .

Pick three people from the past of whom you were afraid. . . Throw their images in a heart in front of you and blow them up. . .

Pick three people who in the future could make

you afraid. . . Throw their images in a heart in front of you and blow them up. . .

Gather up all the neutralized energy and pull it into the Crown Chakra. . . Pull the energy into your energy Body. . .and out to the edges of your Aura.

Be in the center of your head.

Come out of trance.

Bend over.

#72 EXERCISE   Cosmic energy. . .light purple
Inadequacy   Earth energy. . .lavender

Sit in your trance position.

Close your eyes.

Be in the center of your head.

Go into trance.

Ground yourself.

Run your energy.

Create a large box in the center of the room. . .
Starting with your First Chakra at the the
base of your spine. . .throw all the pictures
that you have about how inadequate you are
on a survival level. . . Then do the same at
your Second Chakra. . .the pictures about
your emotional inadequacies. . . The your
Third Chakra. . .inadequate power pictures
. . . The Heart Chakra. . .the pictures dealing
with your abilities of giving and receiving love
. . . Then your Fifth Chakra. . .how well
prepared do you feel within the context of
your communication with others. Go to your
Sixth Chakra and throw all the pictures that
deal with your visual or intellectual inadequacies into the box in front of you. . . Now your
Seventh Chakra. . . your inadequacies dealing
with faith or Spiritual surrender. . . Throw all
these pictures in the box. . .and blow the box

up, neutralizing the energy. . . Send back energy that is not yours to those it belongs to . . . Gather the remaining neutralized energy in front of you. Change that energy into seven pictures that say *I'm okay*. . . Pull these pictures into the Crown or your head and leave one in each of your Major Body Chakras . . . Practice *I'm okay* on all levels.

Be in the center of your head.

Come out of trance.

Bend over.

#73 EXERCISE
Constricted
  Communication

Cosmic energy. . .sky blue
Earth energy. . .rose pink

Sit in your trance position.

Close your eyes.

Be in the center of your head.

Go into trance.

Ground yourself.

Run your energy.

Create a heart in front of you. . . Take any constricting pictures in your Throat Chakra that say *Nice people do not say negative things. Nice people do not get angry. Nice people always say nice things.* . .and throw these pictures into the heart. . . Free yourself from any opinions that are constricting your communication with others. . . Throw all these pictures into the heart. . . Blow it up. . .

Take the neutralized energy and bring it back into your Body. . . Pull it into your Aura. . . Give yourself permission to express yourself.

Be in the center of your head.

Be here.

Come out of trance.

Bend over.

#74 EXERCISE
Speaking for
Someone Else

Cosmic energy. . .sky blue
Earth energy. . .copper

Sit in your trance position.

Close your eyes.

Be in the center of your head.

Go into trance.

Ground yourself.

Run your energy.

Go up in the corner and look back at your Throat Chakra. . . Any energy that is not yours will show up as dark. . . Notice whether there is the energy of another around your Throat Chakra. . . Are you talking for someone else?. . . Are you saying things that express the ideas of another?

Be in the center of your head. . . Take all that energy from around your throat and send it into a heart in front of you. . . all the ideas and thoughts of others. . .get rid of all the pictures and energy around your throat: the communication center. . . Now release the energy in front of you. . . Send energy that belongs to others back to them. Take all the energy that is yours. . .neutralized. . .and pull it into the Crown of your head. . .pull it all the way into yourself. . .your Aura.

Be in the center of your head.
BE YOURSELF.
Comeout of trance.
Bend over.

#75 EXERCISE
Seeing

Cosmic energy. . .sky blue
Earth energy. . .light green

Sit in your trance position.

Close your eyes.

Be in the center of your head.

Go into trance.

Ground yourself.

Run your energy.

Place a heart in front of you and throw the questions, *"Who in my past did not want me to see them? Why?"* into the heart. . . As the questions meet the heart your answers will appear. . . Blow up those images. . .

Throw the questions, *"Who in my present does not want me to see them. . .to see who they really are? Why?"* into the heart. . . Blow up these images.

Throw all the *I can't see* and *Don't see* pictures that you have around your Sixth Chakra into the heart in front of you and change it into your highest level of understanding. . . Pull this understanding into the Crown of your head. . . Allow yourself to see and understand . . .energy. . .

Be in the center of your head.

Have your full potential vision.

Come out of trance.

Bend over.

#76 **EXERCISE**   Cosmic energy. . .light purple
Religion   Earth energy. . .green

Sit in your trance position.

Close your eyes.

Be in the center of your head.

Go into trance.

Ground yourself.

Run your energy.

From around your Seventh Chakra notice if you
have views about God that are not yours. . .
Throw them into a heart in front of you. . .
Blow them up. . . Give yourself the freedom
to know God on your own terms.

Bring the neutralized energy into your Body. . .
Now raise your energy to gold. . . Posulate
that you are bringing in gold energy and that
you *are* gold energy. . . Have your own faith
. . .your own surrender. . .your own connection.

Be in the center of your head.

Come out of trance.

Bend over.

HEALING YOURSELF

Whole Health can be described as existing when your energy is flowing within a constant ebb and flow of movement. Stuck or blocked energy demands that you actively and specifically heal that particular area. Because of the nature of energy concerning its vibration, the energy that moves slowly and gets blocked or stuck very often slows down enough to manifest on a physical level as a cold, tumor, broken leg, depression, cancer etc. Whether your blocks are on a physical or psychic level, you will find the following methods of healing them helpful to you.

METHODS OF SELF HEALING

BREATH AND RHYTHM

Different emotions and other stress situations can constrict your chest and therefore your breathing. This exercise will help your body find a rhythm of inhaling and exhaling: pulling in and letting go.

#77 EXERCISE   Cosmic energy . . . light green
Healing With   Earth energy . . . light green
  Breath And Rhythm

Sit in your trance position.

Close your eyes.

Go into trance.

Ground yourself.

Be in the exact center of your third chakra and breath into that point.

Inhale.

Exhale.

Inhale.

Exhale.

Inhale.

Exhale.

Do your breathing for five to ten minutes with a perfect rhythm, never pausing between the intake and outtake. You may wish to postulate that each "inhale" brings you health or well being and that each "exhale" lets go of illness or stuckness.

Be in the center of your head.

Come out of trance.

Bend over.

SOUND

The vibrational levels of sounds are very strong. Sound can be used to loosen blocks by gently rocking the energy of the block until it all begins to move. Vocal *tones* and *sounds* tend to stay with you so their effect can often outlast other methods of healing. Whether you are listening to birds singing, water lapping, wind blowing, a child laughing, a person singing, or tibetan prayer bowls and bells, sounds can touch you and help heal you.

#78 EXERCISE
Tone Clean

Cosmic energy... lavender
Earth energy... violet

Sit in your trance position.

Close your eyes.

Be in the center of your heart.

Go into trance.

Ground yourself.

As if there were a pipe from each chakra starting with your first... from your first chakra to your fifth chakra... Open your fifth chakra and allow all the excess and wastes and other peoples energy in your first chakra to come up that pipe and out your fifth chakra in the form of a sound. Go through each of your seven body chakras allowing your self to make sounds and tones that release and let go of your stuck energy and blocks. When you are done cleaning out all seven of your body chakras, SING your name out loud. This will help you balance your chakras.

Be in the center of your head.

Come out of trance.

Bend over.

ALLOW YOURSELF TO BE AROUND SOUNDS THAT ARE PLEASING AND HEALING TO YOU!

VISUALIZATION

You can *visualize* with metaphoric images such as your white blood cells (garbage eaters) are pac-mans eating up your tumor. You can visualize "seeing" a picture of a healthy organ and sending that picture intrapersonally, to the organ that is sick. You can also visualize yourself taking all the sickness and throwing it out of your Body... or down your grounding cord.

#79 EXERCISE
To Heal Yourself with Your Original Essence Energy

Be in the center of your Heart Chakra... Feel yourself as a dot of light... your essence energy ... expanding... and continue to expand... expanding yourself, this light, to fill up your Aura out to the Boundaries... Allow this essence energy to nurture and heal as it glistens and sparkles... allowing all illness and pain to dis-

solve and allow the essence energy to rejuve-
nate every cell in your Body and every particle of energy in your Energy System...BE
YOURSELF...

Be in the center of your head.

Come out of trance.

Bend over.

CHANNELLING

To *channel* energy is simply to bring it through
your energy channels. The energy is usually seen
as a color. Any variation of Earth and Cosmic
energies is appropriate.

#80 EXERCISE
Channelling

Cosmic energy... gold
Earth energy... gold

Sit in your trance position.

Close your eyes.

Be in the center of your heart.

Go into trance.

Ground yourself.

Decide on what part of your Body you need healing.

Run your energy... bring in this vibrant alive
golden energy and instead of channelling it out
your seventh chakra, channel it to the part of
your body where you need healing... Allow
this energy to bring whole health back to this
part of your body. Channel and enjoy for about
ten to fifteen minutes.

Be in the center of your head.
BE YOURSELF.
Come out of trance.
Bend over.

FAITH OR PRAYER HEALING

The object of this type of healing is organizing every cell in your body to want and believe in the healing at the same moment. To some this is done with prayer, to others with Faith or Belief.

#81 EXERCISE   Cosmic energy...pink gold
Faith Healing   Earth energy...gold

Sit in your trance position.

Close your eyes.

Be in the center of your heart.

Go into trance.

Ground yourself.

From the center of your heart find your deepest desire to be whole, healed...take that desire and pass it as if on a relay system to each and every cell in your body.

Experience this desire for wholeness on every cell in your body...Allow yourself to want this wholeness more than anything on this planet. Maintain this energy level for at least ten minutes.

Be in the center of your head.

Come out of trance.

Bend over.

UNCONDITIONAL LOVE AND ACCEPTANCE

When you are able to accept yourself, just the way you are without any judgments or considerations of how you are suppose to be, you will find that your health and well-being will improve.

#82 EXERCISE
Unconditional Love

Cosmic energy. . .rose pink
Earth energy. . .pink

Sit in your trance position.

Close your eyes.

Be in the center of your head.

Go into trance.

Ground yourself.

Run your energy.

There is a dot of light in your Heart Chakra. . .
Be that dot of light. . . Allow it to be you with total unconditional love and acceptance for yourself. . . Now expand that light. . . As the light expands any judgments within your Energy System dissolve... Let go of all judgment and open up to complete acceptance of yourself. . . Allow that light to expand to the size and shape of your Human Aura. . . Totally accept yourself, without conditions. . .

Be in the center of your head.

Come out of trance.

Bend over.

DEVELOPING YOUR
PSYCHIC ABILITIES

Being psychic is having an awareness of energy, within you or around you, of why and how things happen. As is true with anything that you wish to develop, the more you practice, the better you get. The following exercises will help you open up and take control of some of your psychic abilities.

#83 EXERCISE
Permission to be
Psychic

Cosmic energy. . .pink
Earth energy. . .sky blue

Sit in your trance position.

Close your eyes.

Be in the center of your head.

Go into trance.

Ground yourself.

Run your energy.

On your time track. . .follow it noticing the pictures, opinions and judgments that you were given about psychic happenings. . .and psychic abilities. . . Notice where your full potential was shut down. . .

Come back to present time and take any pictures that are in your Aura from your childhood. . . also present time opinions and judgments about you as a psychic (more aware) person . . .and throw them into a heart in front of you. . . Blow them up. . . Gather the neutralized energy in front of you and change it into permission. . .and pull it into your Crown Chakra, giving yourself permission to survive, feel, be, love, communicate, see and have faith. . . Give yourself permission to enjoy yourself as the process of opening up (respond-to) your abilities proceeds. . .

Be in the center of your head.
Be the healthiest, strongest, best you can be.
Come out of trance.
Bend over.

#84 EXERCISE
Psychometry

Cosmic energy. . .sky blue
Earth energy. . .yellow

Sit in your trance position.

Close your eyes.

Be in the center of your head.

Go into trance.

Ground yourself.

Run your energy.

Open up your Hand Chakras and your Arm Channels. . . Psychometry is the ability to *read* an object by touching it. . . Actually you are receiving feelings and pictures that are a part of the energy of the object. . . Relax and allow yourself to see the pictures. . . Who owns the object?. . . Where has it been?. . . How old is it?. . . Who made it?. . . Associate your images with the object. . .

Be in the center of your head.

Come out of trance.

Bend over.

#85 EXERCISE   Cosmic energy. . .sky blue
Feeling Your Emotions   Earth energy. . .copper

Sit in your trance position.

Close your eyes.

Be in the center of your head.

Go into trance.

Ground yourself.

Run your energy.

Be in your Second Chakra. . . Pull yourself down into your emotional center. . . Every time that you start to rise back up to your power, pain, or intellect as an escape, pull yourself back to your emotional center again . . . Feel your feelings. . . Allow yourself to get down to your Second Chakra and feel your feelings. . .whatever they are. . .be with them. . . Stay with what you feel.

Come out of trance.

Bend over.

#86 EXERCISE
Taking Control
of Your Emotions

Cosmic energy. . .gold
Earth energy. . .silver

Sit in your trance position.
Close your eyes.
Be in the center of your head.
Go into trance.
Ground yourself.
Run your energy.
Notice that your emotions are yours, but you are not your emotions. They are the paint, and you are the artist. . . In any given situation you have the ability to feel a full spectrum of Human emotions. . . To take charge and change your emotional reactions takes a strong dose of WILL. . .and determination. . . Although it may be difficult, it is not impossible because it is made up of your energy. . . Your emotional response in any situation is your creative energy. . .and you can change it as you can control and change your energy in any situation. . . This is your freedom. . . responding to your ability to feel and having enough control to feel the full spectrum of emotions. . .
Be in the center of your head.
BE YOURSELF.
Come out of trance.
Bend over.

#87 EXERCISE
Clairsentience

Cosmic energy. . .sky blue
Earth energy. . .green

Sit in your trance position.
Close your eyes.
Be in the center of your head.
Go into trance.
Ground yourself.
Run your energy.
Do this exercise either with a partner, or place
    an image of someone in front of you.
Open up your Second Chakra, and allow the
    other's emotions to come into your Body. . .
    Notice how it feels. . . Be clear if you are
    taking on any of those emotions. . . Are you
    taking in the energy and holding it?. . . Clair-
    sentience is when you can clearly feel the
    emotions of another and have enough control
    over your energy system not to take on their
    emotions (energy). . . Now give them back
    their energy. . . You can snap it back as if it
    were attached to a large rubberband. . .
    Notice how it feels to have a clear Second
    Chakra. . .
KNOW YOURSELF.
Be in the center of your head.
Come out of trance.
Bend over.

#88 EXERCISE
Empathy

Cosmic energy. . .sky blue

Earth energy. . .green

Sit in your trance position.

Close your eyes.

Be in the center of your head.

Go into trance.

Ground yourself.

Run your energy.

Empathy is when you first feel another's emotions and then project those emotions back to the person. . . This is not always an ability. Unless you are totally clear about your energy, you run the risk of projecting back some of your own energy. . .which will tire you and could program the other. . . The ability lies within feeling another's emotions and validating that other on an intimate energy level. . . *"I feel what you are feeling"* . . .and letting go.

Be in the center of your head.

Come out of trance.

Bend over.

#89 EXERCISE   Cosmic energy. . .rose pink
Compassion   Earth energy. . .pink

Sit in your trance position.
Close your eyes.
Be in the center of your head.
Go into trance.
Ground yourself.
Run your energy.
Open up your Heart Chakra and allow yourself
   to make a heart connection with another. . .
   Having compassion is having the ability to
   understand what you are in affinity with. . .
   to truly understand and be validating with
   and connecting to the other. . . When you
   look at another compassionately, you are
   seeing the whole picture, not just what the
   Body is experiencing. . . You also see the
   Spirit levels of choice and free will. Each of us
   has the ability to work out the problems we
   create. . . Compassion is when you both feel
   the problem, and then understand the problem, whose it is, and know that they can work
   it out because you see that it is made up of
   their own energy. . .and each of us can control our own energy.
As you send this message to the other, on an
   energy level you are giving confidence to the

other. . .showing them that we all are capable of fighting our own battles. . .each equal within that framework. . .each able to ultimately cope with our own energy. . .at one with that concept. . .in affinity with the idea that we are all capable of being responsible for our own energy. . .a loving acceptance.

Be in the center of your head.

Come out of trance.

Bend over.

#90 EXERCISE   Cosmic energy. . .yellow gold
Dreams   Earth energy. . .silver gold

At night when you are laying in your bed ready
    to go to sleep. . .
Close your eyes.
Be in the center of your head.
Go into trance.
Ground yourself.
Run your energy.
Drain all excess energy down your Grounding
    Cord. . .and be in your Third Chakra. . .
    Open up your Third Chakra. . .the center for
    energy distribution. . .and leave your Body
    through your Seventh Chakra. . .
When you wake up in the morning. . .remember
    to re-enter your Body through your Seventh
    Chakra and to close your Third Chakra down
    . . . Touch it with your hand. . . Breathe into
    the Chakra.
Be in the center of your head.
Be in present time. . .with full memory of where
    you were.
Come out of trance.

#91 EXERCISE
Taking Control
of Your Dreams

Cosmic energy. . .silver blue
Earth energy. . .copper

As you notice that a dream is not going the way you like it. . .and you become aware of that in the dream or by waking up. . .

Ground yourself.

Run your energy.

Fill your mind with something else. . . Start throwing pictures out that will be of what you want.

If you are there when a child is having a bad dream. . .do not wake them. . . Touch them . . . Kiss them. . . Hug them. . . Even though they are asleep. . .speak into their ear, whisper and tell them that together you will create a new dream, and start talking about a place that they love and people they love. . . Consciously fill up the room with scenes and people making it very real. . . This way you are teaching the child how to change their dreams automatically. . .and eventually autonomously. . .

Take full control of yourself. . .your dreams. . . your night mirrors!

Be in the center of your head.

Come out of trance.

#92 EXERCISE   Cosmic energy. . .silver blue
Telepathy   Earth energy. . .green

Sit in your trance position.

Close your eyes.

Be in the center of your head.

Go into trance.

Ground yourself.

Run your energy.

Sit with a friend opposite you, both in trance.
One should be the sender, and the other the
receiver. . . When you are the receiver, make
a tone of voice for your own voice. . .high
or low. . .loud or quiet. . . Give yourself a
recognizable voice so as to distinguish your
inner voice from the voice of the other.

Have your partner pick out a thought to send.
Every minute, rhythmically, have them think
that thought. . . Take that thought and throw
it at you. . . Allow yourself to receive it. . . Be
open. . . Allow your mind to be open. . . . . .
verbalize about your experiences with each
other.

Change positions and try the other part. . . Are
you a better sender or receiver?. . . Listen to
the thoughts in your head.

Start to be aware of the fact that you are
sending and receiving a wide variety of

thoughts. . .
Be in the center of your head.
Come out of trance.
Bend over.

#93 EXERCISE
Balancing Three Eyes

Cosmic energy. . .yellow
Earth energy. . .yellow

Sit in your trance position.

Close your eyes.

Be in the center of your head.

Go into trance.

Ground yourself.

Run your energy.

From the center of your head. . .notice which eye you look out of most. . . Notice how reality appears to you when you look out of only one eye. . .then just the other eye. . .then both Physical eyes. . . Notice the dichotomies such as left and right, good and bad, black and white, when you look from your right and left eye at the same. . . Now open up your Spirit Eye, the third eye, and look through all three eyes at the same time. Notice how you view reality through all three eyes: Male, Female, Soul.

Be in the center of your head.

Come out of trance.

Bend over.

#94 EXERCISE
Clairvoyance

Cosmic energy. . .light green
Earth energy. . .yellow

Sit in your trance position.

Close your eyes.

Be in the center of your head.

Go into trance.

Ground yourself.

Run your energy.

Any time you need to use your clear vision pull yourself into the center of your head and look from in there. . . If you feel weighted down by emotion lighten your color, and then pull yourself into the center of your head. Open up your Sixth Chakra.

All of the exercises in this book were meant to give you the opportunity to practice your Clairvoyance.

Be in the center of your head.

Come out of trance.

Bend over.

#95 EXERCISE   Cosmic energy. . .silver blue
Clairvoyance   Earth energy. . .copper

Sit in your trance position.
Close your eyes.
Be in the center of your head.
Go into trance.
Ground yourself.
Run your energy.
Close down, like the iris of a camera, your first
     five Body Chakras. Open up your Sixth
     Chakra. Your Seventh is already open with
     energy running through it. . .
Postulate that there is a small ball of energy,
     about the size of a marble in front of your
     Sixth Chakra. . . As that marble of energy
     slowly raises and lowers follow it with your
     Sixth Chakra. . . Then as the marble of
     energy moves slowly to the left. . .and slowly
     to the right. . .follow it again with your Sixth
     Chakra. . . Blow up the marble of energy.
Be in the center of your head.
Come out of trance.
Bend over.

#96 EXERCISE

To Improve Your
Concentration

Cosmic energy. . .blue
Earth energy. . .silver blue

Sit in your trance position.

Close your eyes.

Be in the center of your head.

Go into trance.

Ground yourself.

Run your energy.

Open your eyes and your Sixth Chakra. . . With these three eyes concentrate on a postulated gold dot at about six inches in front of your eyes. . . Keep the attention points of your left eye, your right eye and your Spirit eye all on that fourteen karat gold ball.

Release the gold dot of energy and dissolve it.

Be in the center of your head.

Come out of trance.

Bend over.

#97 EXERCISE
Telekinesis (To Move an Object With Your Mind)

Cosmic energy. . .orange

Earth energy. . .red

Close all doors and windows so there will be no breeze.

Place a feather in front of you, on a table.

Sit in your trance position.

Notice, with your eyes open, exactly where the feather is on the table.

Close your eyes.

Be in the center of your head.

Go into trance.

Ground yourself.

Run your energy.

Close down your first two Chakras, your Fourth Chakra and your Fifth Chakra. . . Open up your Third Chakra and your Sixth Chakra. . . Allow a portion of the energy in your Sixth Chakra to move the energy between you and the feather as if the energy were dominos. . . all lined up next to each other. . . Move one domino after another until you have reached the feather. . . Now move the feather. . . Feel yourself moving that feather — allow all doubt in yourself to drain out through your Grounding Cord.

Be in the center of your head.

Come out of trance.

Bend over.

Open your eyes and notice where the feather is in relationship to where it was when you started.

CREATING YOUR OWN PERSONAL UNIVERSE

Your own personal universe, of which *you* are the one true GOD, starts at the core of your essence in your Heart Chakra and ends at your Aura's boundaries. As you create this universe remember that you have an unlimited choice of possibilities and probabilities as to how you run your energy. . . It is your energy and will always be a manifestation of your Spiritual essence. . .of who you are. There are positive and negative attributes to all creations. . an example is that you may get that fancy sports car, but you also have to pay the gas and upkeep bills. Be prepared to take all parts of the energy formations that you mock up through trance.

To manifest your realities with harmony and balance, always create with:

clarity of mind
purity of heart
and
persevering integrity

#98 EXERCISE
The Perfect You

Cosmic energy. . .orange
Earth energy. . .light orange

Sit in your trance position.

Close your eyes.

Be in the center of your head.

Go into trance.

Ground yourself.

Run your energy.

Create in front of you the PERFECT YOU in every way. . .: the Body. . .mind. . .emotions . . .personality patterns. . . Perfect in every way. . .exactly what you want. . . Now stand up, and walk into this mock-up. . . Allow yourself and this perfect you to be in affinity. . . Be at one with being perfect. . . the perfect you.

Sit down.

Be in the center of your head.

Come out of trance.

Bend over.

Enjoy yourself!

#99 EXERCISE   Cosmic energy. . .violet

How to Integrate   Earth energy. . .violet

   Information or a Character Trait

   into Your Body

Sit in your trance position.

Close your eyes.

Be in the center of your head.

Go into trance.

Ground yourself.

Run your energy.

Place in front of you an image of a heart. . .
   Within this heart place all the ideas, cir-
   cumstances and consequences of what you
   need to integrate into the heart. . . Take the
   heart and pull it into your Seventh Chakra. . .
   Pull it all the way down into your feet,
   allowing every cell in your Body to pull some
   of the energy from the heart. . .to bring in the
   information. . .

Be in the center of your head.

BE YOURSELF.

Come out of trance.

Bend over.

#100 EXERCISE
Money

Cosmic energy. . .royal blue
Earth energy. . .copper

Sit in your trance position.
Close your eyes.
Be in the center of your head.
Go into trance.
Ground yourself.
Run your energy.
Postulate that you are surrounded with money
. . . Money is being dumped all over you in
great quantities. . . Money is raining down
over you. . . This money is coming to you
because you are doing something worthwhile
. . .and you are appreciated for it. . . You are
receiving money because you know that your
work is valuable to those who have received
your services (product). . . Allow yourself to
have this money. . . Pull it into yourself. . .
Allow this wealth to drip off of every cell in
your Body.
Be wealth.
Be in the center of your head.
Come out of trance.
Bend over.

#101 EXERCISE
How to Create and
Manifest a Mock-up

Cosmic energy. . .turquoise

Earth energy. . .lavender

Sit in your trance position.

Close your eyes.

Be in the center of your head.

Go into trance.

Ground yourself.

Run your energy.

Go up to your 9th or 10th Chakras and figure out what you want. . .

Go up to your 9th or 10th Chakras and figure out what you want. . . Be sure that you really want it because you may be stuck with it for lifetimes. . .

Get a detailed picture of what you want. . .a clear idea (mock-up) of what it is for you to be in the middle of what you want. . . experiencing exactly all the sides of what you want.

Pull it into your Seventh Chakra, and know it . . .every detail.

Pull it down into your Sixth Chakra and look at it; learn to recognize it.

Pull it into your Fifth Chakra and talk to it; make it into a positive affirmation.

Pull it down into your heart, and be in affinity

with it; be at one with allowing yourself to have it.

Pull it into your Third Chakra. Create a large pink balloon in front of you, outside of your Human Aura, and throw all the pictures, images, impressions and affirmations connected with what you want from your Third Chakra into the balloon.

Let go of the balloon.

Be in the center of your head.

Come out of trance.

Bend over.

Recognize and appreciate it when it comes to you!

#102 EXERCISE Cosmic energy. . .bright yellow
  Create the Job   Earth energy. . .orange
    of Your Dreams

Sit in your trance position.
Close your eyes.
Be in the center of your head.
Go into trance.
Ground yourself.
Run your energy.
Go up in your Ninth Chakra and create the job
    of your dreams. Choose something that you
    would enjoy doing. . .something that you
    would enjoy every part of. . .the hours you
    work. . .the pay you want. . .the type of
    people that you would like to work with. . .
    When you have created exactly what you
    want as a job, pull the picture of it down
    thru the Crown of your head. . . Look at it
    while it passes through your Sixth Chakra,
    say hello to it when it passes through your
    Fifth Chakra. . . Be in affinity with it while it
    passes through your Heart Chakra. . . While
    it is in your Third Chakra create a large pink
    balloon and place the perfect job picture in it
    and project it out into the Universe. . . This
    covers the psychic level. . . All you need to do
    now is listen and look so that you can

recognize it when it comes to you.
Be in the center of your head.
Come out of trance.
Bend over.

#103 EXERCISE   Cosmic energy. . .silver blue
Your Life's Work   Earth energy. . .light orange

Sit in your trance position.
Close your eyes.
Be in the center of your head.
Go into trance.
Ground yourself.
Run your energy.
Create an outline of a heart in front of you. . .
place all the experiences, habits and hobbies
that you enjoy in that heart. . .place all of
your abilities and disabilities in that heart. . .
place all the information you know and life's
experience that you have in that heart. . .
allow that heart to be a light pink energy. . .
allow your Heart Chakra to be a light pink
energy, thus allowing you to be in affinity
with the outcome. . . Throw the question
"What is my Life's Work?" into that heart. . .
allow the energy to create in front of you. . .
allow yourself to have the answer.
Pull the energy of your Life's Work into your
Body and become it. . .allow yourself to have
all your experiences, habits and hobbies. . .
abilities and disabilities. . .your information
and experiences. . .
Be in the center of your head.

BE YOURSELF.
Come out of trance.
Bend over.

UNIT II

THE WHOLE

Now that you *know yourself* and have some basic control of your personal reality, you are ready to look at and understand the WHOLE, of which you and all others are a part.

Chapter Six

COLLECTIVE REALITY

THE ASTRAL PLANES OF REALITY
ASTRAL PROJECTION
TIME TRAVEL

COLLECTIVE REALITY

You exist with all others nestled into a Collective Set of Realities which is continuously created, manifested, and maintained by those Souls who inhabit them. Because of the *law of magnetism* (like energy attracts like energy), in your day to day living you attract the people and situations whose pictures mostly reaffirm yours, as yours do theirs. The entire *Collective Reality* is held together by this type of mutually reaffirming agreement.

There are Seven Planes of energy, each vibrating at seven different levels. You could think of these Planes of energy as you would a large house with many large rooms. Each room is divided only by the vibration of its energy. The lower levels are slowly moving, dense and are physical. The higher levels are vibrating quickly, finely and are etheric.

When first viewing the *Astral Planes* you will notice that there are many forms of energy that might confuse you. There are Souls, such as yourself, attached to their Bodies. There are also Souls that are disembodied. There are whispers of old thoughts and memories left on the ethers that look like monsters, and Souls attached to the Earth because of their greed or attachment who look like ghosts. There are great Deities created out of religious thoughts, and hideous devils created out of fear. Your protection and safety is within the *law of seniority* (you are senior in your space). You will notice that your power to create on the Astral is as strong as your ability to imagine or postulate, because on this level the power is within your postulations. Whatever you postulate to be true is true... only if you truly believe it is.

THE SEVEN ASTRAL PLANES

1. MATERIAL PLANE is made up of all physical life, all physical and material things, and all physical places. Your physical Body exists here.

2. PLANE OF FORCES is made up of the forces that create the charge that you experience.

3. MENTAL PLANE is made up of all mental activity... Group Mind.

4. ASTRAL PLANE is the etheric world, the level of Souls traveling out of Body, disembodied Souls, and Souls in dream states.

5. PLANE OF SOUNDS are all the sounds and tones made by all people and all things.

6. UNITY PLANE collective grouping, Group Memory.

7. PLANE OF OMNIPOTENCE is all that is and one at the same time.

COLLECTIVE REALITIES

planes/levels	1	2	3
7 **PLANE OF OMNIPOTENCE**	**ALL THAT IS**		**AND ONE**
6 **UNITY PLANE**	collective negativity...some Souls send themselves here in dreams (nightmares) or between lives as a self induced punishment (to some people this would be considered "Hell")		groups formed from sets of collective opinions
5 **PLANE OF SOUNDS**	the sounds of negative actions	the sounds of thoughtless and selfish actions	sounds from everyday life of verbal talking
4 **ASTRAL PLANE**	decaying Astral Shells (Bodies) which may appear as monsters	disembodied Souls who are bound to the Earth by negativity and may appear as "ghosts"	disembodied Souls who are bound to the Earth by their attachments and may appear as "ghosts"
3 **MENTAL PLANE**	low negative thoughts that tear up and destroy	old thoughts old attachments	thoughts of mundane daily happenings
2 **PLANE OF FORCES**	apathy, grief loss, pathos boredom	agression, anger, hate, fear, jealousy	passion
1 **MATERIAL PLANE**	decaying physical Bodies	decaying personal physical creations	decaying shared physical creations
	LOWER LEVELS		

COLLECTIVE REALITIES

4	5	6	7
AT THE SAME TIME			
groups that family together	collective creativity (some may create a shared "Heaven" here)	Akashic Records: Group Memory	
sounds of every-day life of non-verbal talking (telepathy)	happy and pleasant sounds nature sounds	"Astral" music	the sound of the WHOLE: Group Voice
day dreams	meditative (trance) experiences	night dreams	resting place for Souls be-tween lifetimes
thoughts of everyday life experiences	high ethical thoughts	high aspirations	Group Mind
self-oriented pleasures and experiences	other-oriented pleasures and experiences: love joy	bliss	Nirvana Group Affinity
existing physical Bodies	existing personal physical reality	existing shared physical reality	existing Group or Universal physical reality
MIDDLE LEVELS		**HIGHER LEVELS**	

ASTRAL PROJECTION

Any time you find yourself thinking of a place, you are there. Even the slightest attention point, causes you to project a portion of yourself, your consciousness, out of your Body and there, to that place. As you become more aware and conscious of your Astral Travels, and place more concentrated attention on where you are going, you will be more and more there.

Your *Astral Body* appears to be similar in looks to your physical Body, but it is translucent. With this in mind, when you come upon a solid object while out of your Body, do not try to push your Astral Body through this object; allow the object to go through you. The object is of the physical world, and it is made up of energy that is moving quite slowly. Such dense matter or energy offers tremendous resistance to being penetrated, and it binds energy moving through it. You in Astral form are made up of etheric energy. The laws that govern etheric energy allow for different vibrations not to affect each other when they are in the same space. Many things solid or other wise can move through your etheric Astral Body if you do not resist them.

To maintain your commitment to your physical Body, you need to connect your Astral Body to your physical Body. There is a silver cord connected to your Astral Body and grounded into the Crown of your Body's head, and also down through your spine and fused into your grounding cord. With this cord you can Astral Travel through any Astral level at any time period and still have a strong enough connection to come back.

#104 EXERCISE
Projection Out of the Body

Cosmic energy... silver
Earth energy... copper

Sit in your trance position.

Close your eyes and be in the center of your head.

Ground yourself.

Run your energy.

Be up in the corner. Notice that there is a silver cord attaching the Astral Body to the Physical Body. This cord has the abilities of rubber... It can stretch out for light years... or be from you in the corner to you in the Body.

Now be in the center of your head.

Project yourself into another chair in the room... Psychically sit in that chair... Feel that chair as you sit on it... Notice what your Body looks like from your view from the chair... Be in the center of your head... Pull yourself all the way into your Body... Now project yourself to be in front of your Body... Notice what the room looks like from this view... Be in the center of your head... This time project yourself to be behind your Body... What does the room look like from this view... Be in the center of your head.

Be up on the roof... Pull yourself, your consciousness, up on the roof... Notice the sky... the view...

Be back in the center of your head.

Be at the beach... Feel the sand, smell the salt air, feel the breeze on your skin... Then be in the center of your head... Pull yourself completely back into the center of your head.

Pick a friend that you wish to visit... Be in your friend's room... Notice the details: the windows and furniture, where your friend is. Choose some method of letting your friend know you are there... whisper something... move something...

Now be in the center of your head...

Be here, in your physical Body.

BE YOURSELF.

Come out of trance.

Bend over.

#105 EXERCISE
Projection Through The Astral Levels

Cosmic energy... copper
Earth energy... light green

Sit in your trance position.

Close your eyes.

Be in the center of your head.

Go into trance.

Ground yourself.

Run your energy.

Now that you are familiar with leaving your Body
and returning to your Body and have a good
sense of the silver cord that attaches you to your
Body...it is time to visit the Astral levels.

Now lower the rate of vibration of your energy...
Keep lowering it until you feel a dampness in the
air... This is the lowest of the lower energies...
This is graveyard energy... Along the strata of
lower levels you will see much negativity and
decay...To keep yourself safe, be in total *nonresistance*... Allow anything or anyone who
frightens you on these lower levels to pass
through you, as if you were not even there
...You can see how dangerous it would be for
you to match energy with any one of these lower
levels ...

Raise the vibration of your energy...Postulate that
your energy is raising...moving faster...A large
part of your everyday life is spent in these middle
Astral levels... On the Mental Plane you will
notice that there are thoughts that are almost as
alive as Beings... There seem to be Beings
everywhere...most are too preoccupied with
their creations to even notice you... In these
middle levels you will see the ethers you day-
dream ... These ethers seem almost like
magic...With just a thought or a strong feeling

you can manipulate and create anything you want... With no more than an inclination you can Astrally visit a friend...

Now raise the vibration of your energy to a gold. Pull every cell up to gold ...You are now approaching the upper Astral levels ... There seems to be a great deal of light in these levels ...Laughter and music can be heard as you pass from one plane to another ... and then to the Group Mind ... Notice the vast amount of data collected here ... Now you notice the Souls asleep all resting ... Now to the great Akashic Records, the Group Memory of all who have and are and will exist. If you are ever having trouble reading someone ... go up to the Akashic Records and look for your information here ...

And raise your energy high enough to notice the white gold energy of the Plane of Omnipotence. Allow yourself for a moment to surrender to this highly pure creative essence...

Now lower your energy and come back into your Body...

Be in the center of your head.

Bring every cell in your Body into present time.

BE YOURSELF.

Come out of trance.

Bend over.

TIME TRAVEL

You have to be aware of and consider not only which Astral level you are visiting, but you must also know and understand which time frame you are in; the past, present or future.

Although you can Astral travel into the past, you can not change it. The only point in time you can instantaneously control is the time, reality, and Body that your silver cord is attached to. Your present time Body and reality is the key to the creative manifestation of your Soul here in the physical plane. The past you can visit to experience, understand, and reexperience your past and the pasts of others. The future you can visit to experience the probable and possible futures of you and others. These projections will not change the future for you. Your future is created by your present time thoughts, daydreams and fantasies.

#106 EXERCISE
Time Travel

Cosmic energy ... silver blue
Earth energy ... copper

Sit in your trance position.

Close your eyes.

Be in the center of your head.

Go into trance.

Ground yourself.

Any time that you are thinking of the past or the possibilities of the future, you are in part Time Traveling ... Part of you is there ... The amount of your energy and consciousness that you take with you is in direct proportion to your ability to BE where you want to BE ...

Practice being in the center of your head ... then traveling to a past incident ... Pick a time you want to remember ... and be there ... you will notice that you move on this level with super-luminal speed ... Remember to be aware of the details of where you are ... then back into the center of your head ... and then into the probable and possible futures ... As you travel in the past and future you will notice that you cannot create change for any other lifetimes except this present one. Your Soul can only control the Body that the silver cord is connected to ... the one in the present moment.

Come back into present time ...

Bring every cell in your Body into this present moment.

Be in the center of your head.

Come out of trance.

Bend over.

Chapter Seven

YOUR RELATIONS WITH OTHERS

ENERGY EXCHANGES
AND COMMUNICATIONS

Each Human Being has their own style of communicating with another. Some styles enhance the relations and intimacy with another and some styles restrict and inhibit these relations.

One of the first and most primary lessons when you communicate with another is for you to be in the center of your own head, and *not* in the center of the other's head. Any time that your curiosity gets the better of you, and you wonder about someone—what makes them do a particular thing, or think a certain way—you have projected yourself into the other's head. This will cause a great deal of confusion or pain for them. It could also cause a great deal of confusion for you because you will be viewing the world through the eyes of the other. If you do not know that this is what is happening, then you start to lose your sense of identity.

In order to re-establish your own viewpoint, gently pull yourself back into the center of your own head. Pull all your attention to behind your eyes, and then ask your questions, and have your curiosity. Conversely, when someone is in your head and it feels as if they were stomping around inside, you can ask them to pull their attention back into their own head. If the other person appears not to understand it, simply place your fingertips

together, and you will create a strong vortex of your
own energy which will kick the other out.

RESISTANCE, AFFINITY, AND NONRESISTANCE

When you are communicating and relating with
another, both of you are throwing energy to the
other. You have three styles in which you can
receive or embrace the energy of the other: to **resist**
it, to be in **affinity** with it, or to **nonresist.**

RESISTANCE: The energy in your Aura and your
Body tightens and becomes rigid in
order to use force to actively fight
off or oppose the energy that is
coming into you. At this point
every cell becomes a shield, holding that which you resist near you
at the same time that you are
fighting it off.

AFFINITY: The energy in your Aura and every
cell in your Body are in agreement
and at one with the energy coming
to you.

**NON-
RESISTANCE:** The energy in your Aura and
Body is neutral in regard to the
energy coming to you. There is no
force; no agreement. You notice
the energy coming to you, and you

watch the energy go through you and out the other side of you. You have no considerations or judgments on which it will get caught.

#107 EXERCISE
Releasing Resistance
And Experiencing Nonresistance

Cosmic energy ... yellow
Earth energy ... orange

Sit in your trance position.

Close your eyes.

Be in the center of your head.

Go into trance.

Ground yourself.

Run your energy.

Postulate that all the energy in your Aura, your Chakras or your circuitry that is in resistance is brown ...

Allow your feet to relax and the brown resistant energy to flow out your Feet Chakras ... Let go of all the resistance in your ankles ... in your calves ... Let go of any resistance in your pelvic cradle ... Allow the resistance to go down your grounding cord ... any resistance to your own survival ... Let go of any resistance that you hold around your sex organs ... Let go of all the resistance you have for sitting in the chair ... Let go of any resistance you have for your emotions ... for your power ... Let go of all the resistance around your heart ... your resistance to being loved and loving ... Let go of all the resistance in your back ... Allow it to drain out your grounding cord and into the center of the Earth ... Let go of the resistance in your neck ... to communicating your thoughts or feelings ... Let go of all the resistant energy in your throat and from off of your face ... Let go of all the resistance you have towards smiling or frowning ... Let go of the resistance on the top and back of your head...

Postulate that you are totally nonresistant ... Postulate that there are large waves of water pounding through you ... You are nonresistant to them ... Now postulate that sunlight is shining through you ... now darkness ... It goes right through you ... Postulate that a person could walk up to you and walk right through you ... You are in neutral and totally nonresistant.

Be in the center of your head.

Come out of trance.

Bend over.

#108 EXERCISE
Resist, Affinity
And Nonresistance (to do with a partner)

Cosmic energy . . . blue
Earth energy . . . silver blue

Sit in your trance positions opposite each other.

Both close your eyes.

Both be in the center of your own heads.

Both go into trance.

Both ground yourselves.

Both run your own energy.

One of you be "A" and the other be "B"

"A" pick something that you don't like about
   "B" . . . it could be as simple as their watch or
   hair color . . . send "B" that negative message
   on an energy level by throwing them a picture, and emotion, or a thought. . .

"B" you are first to **resist** the negative message
   . . . how do you feel when you resist a negative
   message? . . . "A" how do you feel when you
   send a negative message and "B" resists it? . . .

Next "B" you are to be in **affinity** with the
   negative message . . . how does this make you
   feel? . . . "A" how do you feel when "B" is in
   affinity with your negative message?

Lastly "B" you are to **nonresist** the negative
   message . . . allow it to go through you . . .
   how does this feel? "A" how does it feel to you

when "B" is nonresistant to your negative message?

Now "A" chose a compliment or positive mes-message to send to "B" ... "B" you are to first **resist** that positive message ... then you are to be in **affinity** with it ... and then **nonresist** it ... again notice how you react or feel with each way of receiving the energy.

Change places and "B" you are the sender and "A" you are the receiver...

When you are done:

Be in the center of your own head.

BE YOURSELF.

Come out of trance.

Bend over.

Verbalize with each other about your reactions to the exercise.

COMMUNICATION CORDS

When you and another communicate, you throw energy *cords* to each other. These cords are definite lines of energy. An analogy for a cord would be a telephone wire. For just like a telephone wire, a cord carries information and messages between people. It acts like a channel for the pictures to be sent and received. They go from your Chakras to the Chakras of the other person.

You have control over where you throw your cords and where you receive other's cords. Or, you may wish not to receive a certain cord at all, letting it go right through you.

Any message from the cords chart can be sent from, or received into your Chakras. Please note: A cord does not necessarily go from the First Chakra to another's First Chakra; a cord from any Chakra can be sent to any Chakra. You have complete control of where you send and where you receive all communication cords.

CHAKRA	MESSAGE	CHAKRA
7	*I own you!* *Own me!*	7
6	*I see you!* *See me, pay attention to me!* *I see what you see.* *See for me.* *Let me see for you.*	6
5	*Telepathic messages* *Let me tell you something!* *Tell me something! Talk to me!* *Let me talk for you.* *Talk for me!* *I hear you.* *Hear me!* *I will say what you want to hear.* *Say what I want to hear.*	5
4	*I love you.* *Love me!*	4
3	*I have control of your energy.* *Tell me what to do!* *Take my energy.* *Give me energy.*	3
2	*I feel your emotions.* *Feel my emotions.* *I want to sexually feel you.* *Sexually feel me.*	2
1	*I will save you, keep you alive.* *Save me, keep me alive* *Ground me.* *I will ground you.*	1

SENDING AND RECEIVING
COMMUNICATION CORDS

When you want to communicate with another you simply take your message and throw it from the appropriate Chakra in your energy Body to where you want the other to receive it. The cord should be in harmony with the message sent. The same is true when you receive a cord. Allow the received message to enter the Chakra that will allow full communication with the other. When receiving a cord remember that you may either resist it or be in affinity with it. If you wish not to receive a cord from another, simply nonresist it.

#109 EXERCISE
Cord Sending And
Receiving

Cosmic energy...green
Earth energy...copper

Sit in your trance position.

Close your eyes.

Be in the center of your head.

Go into trance.

Ground yourself.

Run your energy.

Either sit across from a partner, or create a mock-up of a person you relate with often... and have the other throw a cord at you and you notice where you take the cord in...Go through the list of cord messages... Chakra by Chakra and notice how you react to each cord... When your partner says "save me" from their First Chakra, where do you take that cord in?... etc....

After you have been through the lists of cords, remove all the cords and make a separation from your partner... Release and neutralize and retrieve the creative energy you used during this exercise... Pull it back into your Body...

Be in the center of your head.

Come out of trance.

Bend over.

HOW TO RELEASE A CORD

To keep your Chakras open and functioning, you must clean them out and remove any old cords that are not presently valid. By the end of the day, you may have as many as twenty in one Chakra, blocking the Chakra. Cords are neither right nor wrong, positive nor negative. They are either appropriate or inappropriate for you.

#110 EXERCISE   Cosmic energy...sky blue
How to Release   Earth energy...tourquoise
* A Cord*

Sit in your trance position.
Close your eyes.
Be in the center of your head.
Go into trance.
Ground yourself.
Run your energy.
From the center of your head, look down at
    your Chakras... Notice at which Chakras
    you collect most of your cords... What does
    this mean to you?... Starting with your First
    Chakra... allow the energy from your back
    channels to gently push the cords, one at a
    time, from your First Chakra... Never force
    a cord out, nor pull a cord out... Be gentle
    and easy with yourself... Go up each Chakra

pushing the cords out to the edges of your Boundaries... releasing the cord. Be sure that wherever the cord was, you have filled up that space with your own energy...

After cleaning all your cords out, you may want to reinstate cords that you especially desire, such as heart cords to loved ones, survival cords to an infant.

Be in the center of your head.

Come out of trance.

Bend over.

MATCHING PICTURES: MATCHING ENERGY

The essence of relationship is diversity: each individual has something different to offer the other. To be stuck in a *matching picture* is to be stuck in a mutual misinterpretation of each other. Both of you may assume that you are alike and therefore completely *match each others energy* (act alike). When this happens you will both experience a loss of originality and individuality.

Matching pictures are the matching beliefs or perceptions which different individuals may share. This set of matching pictures is stuck when the match is equivalent of looking at a mirror image of yourself, for both of you.

MERGING AURAS

Merging Auras happen when you and another are mutually stuck on a matching picture. The pictures in both of your Auras migrate to the edge of both of your Auras. The amount of charge they both give off eventually dissolves both Boundaries. At that moment energy from each Aura pours into the Aura of the other. Eventually you share one large merged Aura and one set of Boundaries. You are no longer two free individuals relating. Instead you are stuck in a mutually validating process that reaffirms the agreement that you are both the same because at this point both of your Auras have merged into one Aura ...By not allowing any other energy in... eventually the energy becomes frozen and the relationship stagnates as well. Because you have forgotten who you are, you assume that you are the other.

#111 EXERCISE
Cosmic energy... sky blue

Matching and Merging Earth energy... lavender

> Sit in your trance position.
>
> Close your eyes.
>
> Be in the center of your head.
>
> Go into trance.
>
> Ground yourself.
>
> Run your energy.
>
> Notice the light in the center of your head... Be that dot of light... Expand that dot of light ... Expand yourself to fill up your Body... As you are doing this find three physical differences between you and the other... Then expand to fill up your Aura to your Boundaries... As you do this find three different energy patterns in your Auras... Then create a strong Boundary.
>
> BE YOURSELF.
>
> Be in the center of your head.
>
> Come out of trance.
>
> Bend over.

ARGUMENTS AND RESOLUTIONS

Because no two people have the same pictures, at times it may be hard to find agreement with one another. When this happens, you have two choices: to fight to win, or to resolve.

When the two choose to fight to win, it becomes a contest of who can hurt the other, or who can manipulate best. Insults get passed around and relationships get temporarily severed. Each cares only for themselves. Each protects themselves and tries to prove the other wrong. Even if you think that you have won, you have not because you have lost communication with the other. Both of you are stuck. with Auras that are damaged and fixated. Both will have a *rip* starting at the point in the Aura at which the picture occurred that started the argument. Both will have whacks in their Auras. A *whack* is the energy of invalidation which shows up as a black dot of negative energy. A whack is directed to an already charged picture in your Aura. It may be as overt as an insult, or it may be passed covertly as a tight-lipped look, or as subtly as pure negative energy thrown at a stuck picture.

When the goal in the argument is resolution, the resolving of differences, you are no longer challenged to win. Instead you make the points of disagreement as clear as possible. You always bring the argument and keep the argument to its po-int, (its POsitive INTention). When resolution is the goal, all involved are the winners. There is a sense of fairness and mutual respect.

#112 EXERCISE
Rips and Whacks

Cosmic energy... lavender
Earth energy... purple

Sit in your trance position.

Close your eyes.

Be in the center of your head.

Go into trance.

Ground yourself.

Run your energy.

Go up in the corner and look back down at your
energy Body... Are there any black dots?... If
so, where? Do you hold whacks?... What pictures of yours collect the whacks?... Is there a
rip or tear in your Aura?... If so, what is the
picture involved?

Be back in the center of your head.

Place a heart in front of you... Throw all the
whacks from your Aura into the heart...
Throw the pictures that attracted whacks into
the heart. Throw the picture that caused the
rip into the heart... and release the energy
from the heart in front of you... Neutralize
the energy... and pull it into your Crown
Chakra... filling up all the holes and zipper-
ing up the rip...

Be in the center of your head.

Come out of trance.

Bend over.

SYMPATHY, EMPATHY, COMPASSION

When you find yourself in a situation where you want to get or give help, your good intentions will not outweigh the amount of

	SYMPATHY
WHAT IS IMPLIED	*"I feel your problem. Oh it is such a big problem. Let me have it so that I can solve it for you because you cannot. I give you pity."*
CHANNELING OF ENERGY	*The Second Chakras are hooked up by an energy cord. When you give sympathy, you pull the problem into your Second Chakra through this cord and keep it there. You are stuck with the other's energy.*
OUTCOMES	*If you have taken the problem, you are stuck with it until you realize, if ever, that it is not made up of your energy. Therefore, it is not yours. If you were the one who gave your problems away, you would have to recreate all the situations leading up to them again until you finally completed the cycle yourself.*

damage done by incorrect channeling of your energy. Because the situation (problem, picture, emotion, or illness) is made up of energy, the only person who can solve it is the person who created it. The most important gift you can give anyone is your confidence that they can work out their own problems.

EMPATHY	COMPASSION
"I feel your problem. Because I want to validate you, I will hold up your problem and project it back to you to show you that I understand."	"I feel your problem. I understand how hard it is to work out your problem because sometimes it is hard for me to work out my problems. I have confidence that you can resolve your problem because of the natural laws of energy you can control your own energy and your problems are created out of your energy."
The Second Chakras are hooked up by an energy cord. When you give empathy—or become empathetic—you pull the other's problem into your Second Chakra through the cord. Then you pull the other's problem into your Third Chakra and project it back. Problems may occur if you use too much of your own energy in the projection, changing the structure of the problem.	The Heart Chakras are hooked up with a cord of energy. The understanding you have for the other is gained through affinity. You are at one with the person. Not only do you understand their problem, but you understand the whole person. You understand why they have created their problem and what they are getting out of it. The understanding comes from a broader spectrum: seeing the forest, not just the trees.
If you have been projecting or reflecting back the problem, you will be tired out. It takes effort and energy to project another's pictures or problem. There is also the potential hazard of confused ownership of the problem.	Through an affinity cord you have taught the other true understanding, and you still remain yourself.

#113 EXERCISE
Sympathy, Empathy,
Compassion

Cosmic energy...rose pink

Earth energy...pink

Sit in your trance position.
Close your eyes.
Be in the center of your head.
Go into trance.
Ground yourself.
Run your energy.
Go up in the corner and look at your Body...
   Are you in **sympathy** with anyone?... Look
   for Second Chakra cords and notice if you
   have energy in your Second Chakra that is not
   yours. Notice if you are feeling **empathy** for
   anyone: Look for Second Chakra cords and a
   projection screen in front of your Third
   Chakra.
Now throw all these energy formations and the
   reaffirming pictures into a heart in front of
   you... Send all energy that belongs to the
   other back to them... and release and
   neutralize the energy you had tied up within
   the exchange... Replace all sympathy and
   empathy cords with Heart Chakra cords for
   sending and receiving **compassion**.
Fill up any holes in your Chakras or Aura with
   your own energy.
Be in the center of your head.
BE YOURSELF.
Come out of trance.
Bend over.

#114 EXERCISE
Cosmic energy... orange
Sympathy,
Earth energy... light orange
Empathy, Compassion (to do with a partner)

Sit in your trance positions opposite each other.
Both close your eyes.
Both be in the center of your own heads.
Both go into trance.
Both ground yourselves.
Both run your own energy.
One of you be "A" and one of you be "B".
"A" pick a problem that you have... and send it on an energy level to "B"... send your problem with the desire to get **sympathy**... "B" go into sympathy with "A"...how does it feel to receive sympathy and how does it feel to give sympathy?
"A" still throw that problem at "B"... "B" now empathize with "A"... how does it feel to receive **empathy**?... how does it feel to give empathy?...
"A" still send your problem, and "B" go into a compassionate posture with "A"... what does **compassion** do for both of you?
Change positions and "B" pick a problem and send it to "A"... go through the exercise with the roles changed.
When you are done:
Be in the center of your own head.
BE YOURSELF.
Come out of trance.
Bend over.
Verbalize with each other about your reactions to the exercise...

KARMA

Taking a Body on the Planet Earth is like en-rolling in a very large Spiritual School. Here you the Soul have the freedom to try out many styles of Be-ing to learn many lessons in many creative fashions: to be who you want to be, act as you want to act, and do what you want to do, and to do all of this with whom you want. There is only one law: the *law of responsibility*—if it is your energy, it's your problem. For every movement or action you make, you create a cycle of your energy that will eventual-ly come back to you for completion. The comple-tion of a cycle is considered to be your *Karma*, a mirror or reflection of how you act or the deeds you do. If you identify yourself as a Body, it seems as if you are thrown into a punishment for every nega-tive act and a reward for every positive act. From a Spiritual sense, Karma is a study in dichotomies: a lesson on how it feels to experience both sides of any action.

#115 EXERCISE
Karma

Cosmic energy... violet
Earth energy... rose pink

Sit in your trance position.

Close your eyes.

Be in the center of your head.

Go into trance.

Run your energy.

Go up in the corner, and look back down at the Aura around your Body. Notice your unfinished cycles... as if they were each a deck of cards, fanned out with certain cards missing... Notice the amount of energy you use to keep those incomplete decks of cards in your Aura... Notice where you hold them; notice how much space they take up... Notice the type of person you need to be around because of the original act... Notice how much of your creativity is invested in these cycles.

Be in the center of your head... Place a heart in front of you, and let it represent one of your cycles... Throw an important question at the heart... What do you need to do to complete this cycle? Allow your answer to appear...

Be in the center of your head.

Come out of trance.

Bend over.

CONTRACTS

A *contract* is a fixed energy agreement. You have a
contract with each relationship that you have,
whether it is extremely intimate, surface, long term
or short term. A contract is created from the pictures
that both (or all) of you offer to the relationship.
These pictures include not only the needs, expectations, and probable realities of those concerned, but
also the limitations that you have for that relationship. Even though a contract is somewhat like a
covenant, it can be changed. As your ability to relate
develops, you will take a conscious look at contracts
as they are made.

#116 EXERCISE
Contracts

Cosmic energy... yellow gold
Earth energy... silver blue

Sit in your trance position.

Close your eyes.

Be in the center of your head.

Go into trance.

Run your energy.

Choose a relationship that you would like to understand better... Raise your level of energy up to a Unity level... very high up... Keep raising your energy until you reach that group mind, Unity Plane... When you have reached this Plane of energy... project yourself out to the 6th, and 7th levels to the Akashic Records (group memory)... It may appear as a library, a palace, a record book... It appears to you as you can have it... Ask to see your contract with the person of your choice... Read it with the intent to understand, but not necessarily to change... You cannot change a contract alone because it has energy that belongs to another... and the other has to change their energy...

Be in the center of your head.

Bring every cell in your Body into present time.

Come out of trance.

Bend over.

RELATIONSHIP AURAS

When you and another have an on-going relationship, the energy that both of you put into
relating is continuous enough to create an Aura of
its own. The *Relationship Aura* that you share with
one person will be completely different than the one
you share with another. You will have as many Relationship Auras as you have on-going relationships.

The Relationship Aura will show the power
plays, the level of intimacy allowed within the relationship, the games played to avoid intimacy, the
communication or lack of communication, the
shared pictures, the limitations and the amount of
love they share.

#117 EXERCISE   Cosmic energy... light green
Relationship Aura   Earth energy... copper

Sit in your trance position.

Close your eyes.

Be in the center of your head.

Go into trance.

Ground yourself.

Run your energy.

Choose an on-going relationship that you want to understand and see more clearly... Place an image of you and an image of the other in front of you... And, place a large heart between the two images... Allow this heart to represent the relationship, and allow both images to channel the energy that they put into their relationship into the heart. The heart will take shape and form as the energies flow into it... Notice if there is a grounding cord to the Aura (the relationship commitment), whose energy forms it, the balance of both energies... What shape does the Aura have?

Moving up through the Chakra areas, read the survival and emotional levels, the power plays, the affinity and love levels, the style and amount of communication, the visual understanding and the amount of faith within the relationship... As you do this, continuously notice the balance of energy:... Who has more energy in which areas?...Notice the colors; are the tones dark or light?... Notice the willingness or unwillingness to invest energy...

Release the energy that is in front of you... Turn it into neutral energy... Gather it up and make a large vibrant golden sun out of this neutral energy... Pull it into the Crown of your heads and into your Body... every cell in your Body... and into your Chakras and your Aura... filling yourself up with this vibrant gold energy...

Be in the center of your head.

Bring every cell in your Body into this present moment.

Come out of trance.

Bend over.

HOW TO CHANGE YOUR RELATIONSHIPS WITH OTHERS

Your ability to relate with others will only be as free as you are, or as limited and restricting as you are. What is referred to as the *law of attraction* states that like energy attracts like energy. If you want to change your relationship, or the style of the relationship, change yourself.

#118 EXERCISE Cosmic energy... rose pink
How To Change Earth energy... pink
  Your Relationship With Others

Sit in your trance position.

Close your eyes.

Be in the center of your head.

Go into trance.

Ground yourself.

Run your energy.

Choose a relationship that you want to change in some way... In front of you create an image of both of you... and of the style of relating that you want to change... Notice where you are holding this energy pattern... Which of your pictures reinforce the patterns?... Release the images in front of you.

Create a heart in front of you... Throw the energy into your Aura, Chakras, and Body that you saw reinforcing the patterns that you want to change... into the heart... all the pictures, shields, whacks, and any energy patterns that are restricting your essence energy in the relationship... or any energy of yours that is restricting the other from running their essence energy... Take full responsibility for your own energy, and allow the other to take responsibility for their own energy.

Blow up the heart and neutralize the energy.

Create a heart in front of you... Allow it to represent what you want to know... Take the question. "Where do we go from here?" for the relationship... Throw the question into the heart; and when the answer appears, read it... Then gather the heart and the information you seek and pull it into your Crown Chakra... Pull the information into your Body, Chakras, and Aura... Integrate the information on every level...

Be in the center of your head.

Be your own pure essence energy.

Come out of trance.

Bend over.

Chapter Eight

HOW TO READ
ANOTHER'S ENERGY

PROFESSIONAL ETHICS FOR READING

PROGRAMMING

HOW TO READ ANOTHER FOR YOUR
OWN INFORMATION

HOW TO LOOK FOR ANOTHER'S
ORIGINAL ESSENCE ENERGY

SYMBOLIC READING

HOW TO READ YOU IN RELATIONSHIP
TO ANOTHER

HOW TO GIVE A CLAIRVOYANT
READING

PROFESSIONAL ETHICS FOR READING ANOTHER

Because you are counseling the Soul of another during a reading, you may consider yourself as part of the helping professionals. To establish and maintain a professional attitude you must set a standard for yourself. This standard must allow you the freedom to remain yourself, and it must encourage the integrity and freedom of your readee. Both you and your readee are open and vulnerable to each other's energy for the duration of the Reading. You are protected by your ability to know yourself. The readee is only protected by the integrity you have towards a high set of ethics.

The following code of ethics is the standard that the Readers and Healers at Heartsong use as their guidelines.

HEARTSONG'S CODE OF ETHICS

- I will take full responsibility for my own energy. I will set it and run it accordingly.
- I will take the time to ground myself.
- I am committed to being in my Body experiencing the present moment.
- I am emotionally neutral and am always aware of which energy is mine and which is not.
- I will not undermine another by taking on their problems; I create no dependencies. Instead, by example, I will teach the laws of autonomy and free will.
- I will not use my abilities to control, manipulate or program another.
- I will use my clairvoyance to see the TRUTH for each person and not to be mischievous.
- I will read the past and present with only a reference to the probable and possible futures of another: thus allowing the other the freedom to create their own future.
- I will look for the way in which it is easiest for the other to have the energy, and I will communicate to that po-int (positive intention).
- Because I have a strong heart connection with another, I see the other as an equal Human Being, subject to the respect that a physical and spiritual Being deserves.
- I allow others the privacy sacred to all SOULS.
- I devote my life to the purity and truth of my own essence within my own heart, as well as helping others find their own purity and truth within their own hearts.
- I will devote myself to the individuality of each soul, respecting that individuality in its search for health, well-being and ultimately, GOD.

PROGRAMMING

Many people are very open to the opinions and pictures of another. They are easily *programmed* by the pictures they are sent. If you are talking to someone who seems to be losing their space and freedom to the pictures you are sending, pull your pictures back. To tell if this is happening, simply close your eyes for a second and look at a gauge which represents how programmable the other is. The degrees above 70 will show you how programmable the other is; and the degrees under 30 will show you how resistant and closed the other is. The region of balance and autonomy is 30 to 70. Within the middle region, the person is discriminating what is appropriate for them to take in and what to throw out. This person has their *free will*.

HOW TO READ ANOTHER'S ENERGY FOR YOUR OWN INFORMATION

When reading another for your own information and clarity, remember it is just that: for your own information. Unless the person has come to you for your views or a Reading, you would be intruding and invading their space by trying to push unasked for information on them.

#119 EXERCISE   Choose a color a few shades
How To Read Another   lighter than the one
of the person you are reading.

Sit in your trance position.

Close your eyes.

Be in the center of your head.

Go into trance.

Ground yourself.

Run your energy.

Clean yourself out, and notice your energy... Where are you?... How do you feel?... What pictures are you stuck on?...

Ask yourself what the reason is for reading this person... What do you want to know?... What is your intent?... What do you need and want from the reading?

Find neutrality, and keep it.

Close down your 1st, 2nd, 3rd, 4th, 5th, and 7th

Chakras...

Open up your 6th Chakra for clear vision.

Create an image of the person outside your Boundaries, in front of your 6th Chakra...

Take the questions you have... or the confusion
you have about that person, and throw them into the image. The combined energies will light
up the picture and energy patterns around the
image of the person that have to do with your
questions... Read and translate the Aura, Chakras, pictures: looking at the different qualities of
the energy pattern...

Let go of the reading.

Be in the center of your head.

Come out of trance.

Bend over.

HOW TO LOOK FOR ANOTHER'S ORIGINAL ESSENCE

To truly understand another you must look at who the other is beyond all their self restricting energy patterns. It is important to go to the *original essence*, the energy essence prior to their first incarnation on Earth.

#120 EXERCISE
How To Look For
Another's Original Essence

Cosmic energy... violet

Earth energy... rose pink

Sit in your trance position.

Close your eyes.

Be in the center of your head.

Go into trance.

Ground yourself.

Run your energy.

Place a clear picture of the other's Heart Chakra
in front of you... At the precise center of this
Chakra is the original essence color... Notice
where else that person carries that color.

Release the picture in front of you and replenish
your Aura with the neutralized energy.

Be in the center of your head.

Come out of trance.

Bend over.

SYMBOLIC READING

Symbolic reading is when an arbitrary image becomes a metaphor and is translated into information. You might even wish to understand all clairvoyant reading to be symbolic readings, for even your Aura and Chakras are in fact symbols of who you are.

There are two methods of symbolic reading that you can employ. One is to read a symbol already in the energy Body of another, such as a medical symbol carried by a doctor to psychically state his profession. The other method is to create a symbol of your own to signify certain facts. At Heartsong School we use a heart with wings in this way.

The Heartsong Reading symbolizes a whole person: both physical and spiritual. The heart represents the Body or physical personality. The wings represent the Soul. The attachment of the wings to the heart characterize the twelve levels of consciousness and signify the integration of these levels into the physical reality. Therefore the relationship of the heart to the wings illustrate the balance of spiritual and physical realities. What you are reading is the qualities of energy that are taken on within the limits of the symbol.

#121 EXERCISE
Heartsong Reading

Cosmic energy . . . sky blue
Earth energy . . . turquoise

Sit in your trance position.

Close your eyes.

Be in the center of your head.

Go into trance.

Ground yourself.

Run your energy.

Choose a person to read... place the outline of a heart with wings in front of that person and allow their energy to flow into the symbol; allow their energy to color and shape this symbol... what color is the heart?... How is it shaped... what does the shape mean to you?... Are the wings attached to the heart?... If not which levels are not attached?... What color or colors are the wings?... What does the relationship between the heart and the wings mean to you?

Blow up the symbol.

Be in the center of your head.

BE YOURSELF.

Come out of trance.

Bend over.

HOW TO READ YOURSELF IN RELATIONSHIP TO ANOTHER

When you wish to understand you in relationship to another, you simply need to go into trance and look at the energy between both of you. The combinations of both your energies will form patterns or games for you to interpret.

#122 EXERCISE
Reading You in
Relationship to Another

Cosmic energy . . . sky blue

Earth energy . . . lavender

Sit in your trance position.

Close your eyes.

Be in the center of your head.

Go into trance.

Ground yourself.

Run your energy.

Choose a relationship in which you and the other have some energy plays or games going on... In front of you create an image of you and that person... Look at the cords between you both... Notice where they are being sent and where they are being received... Notice the level of resistance in the Auras... Notice the viewpoints... What pictures are you both looking at in each other?... Are there any matching pictures?... What pictures do you light up in each other?... Look at both Bodies and then look at both your Soul and the Soul of the other... Notice the Bodies' relationships and the Souls' relationships... Are these different?... And lastly look at the contract that you have with that person...

Release the images in front of you, and make a separation.

Be in the center of your head.

BE YOURSELF.

Come out of trance.

Bend over.

HOW TO GIVE A
CLAIRVOYANT READING

The main purpose of Clairvoyant Reading is to provide safe exploration for you and your readee. Usually your readee will light up all the pictures and problems that they want you to read. You are a translator for their information. From a neutral place, uncharged and nonjudgmental, you read the energy Body as you would a book. You translate the energy in the Aura, Chakras and pictures as you are translating the words on this page. Although your readee may be aware of energy, your communication will be clearer if you use vocabulary that your readee will be sure to understand. For example, instead of telling your readee that they are not grounded, tell them that they are not committed to themselves, or to working their problems through.

At all times notice if you are seeing the person clearly or if you are reading yourself. Your clarity about who you are will help you determine this.

Prepared with your techniques and held up by your ethics, you are ready to read.

#123 EXERCISE
How to Give a
Clairvoyant Reading

Choose a color a few
shades above the one
that you are reading

Sit directly across from the one you are reading.

Sit in your trance position.

Close your eyes.

Be in the center of your head.

Go into trance.

Ground yourself and ground your room.

Clean yourself... letting go of your stuck pictures
... opinions... judgments... problems... so that
you can be here in this present moment... committed to this reading.

Run your energy.

Stabilize your energy.

Create a strong boundary around you.

Find neutrality.

Close down the following Chakras: 1st, 2nd, 3rd,
4th, 7th.

Open up your 5th Chakra for verbal communica-
tions and your 6th Chakra for clear vision.

Make a heart connection with the other.

Look at the other and notice: programability
gauge... where is she/he?... why did he/she
want a reading?... Notice the shape and form of
the Aura... the colors... Notice other people's
energy,... blocks... resistance... rips...
valences... boundaries... Now notice the seven

Body Chakras:... Start at the 1st Chakra and read the patterns of male and female energy... the blocks, shields, pictures, colors, cords, whacks... Do this in all the Chakras... then the Aura... Check circuitry and grounding... Are they using their own original essence energy?

Communicate clearly what you are seeing, keeping it simple and to the point.

End your communication by drawing the energy together into one final statement.

Pull any energy that is yours back into your own Aura.

Make a separation (find at least five differences between you and the other).

Blow up any pictures on which you got stuck during the reading.

Clean yourself out.

Come out of trance.

Bend over.

The reading is over. Let go of it.

Chapter Nine

HOW TO HEAL
ANOTHER'S ENERGY

PROFESSIONAL ETHICS FOR HEALING

METHODS OF HEALING

HOW TO GIVE A HEALING

HOW TO HEAL ANOTHER'S ENERGY

An important understanding for you as a healer is that **all healing is self healing**. Your job as a healer is to teach on an energy level. You clean and balance the energy Body of your healee. It is in this way that you show your healee how it feels to be balanced and unblocked. It may take several Healings before your healee can integrate and maintain this change of energy for themselves. Your effectiveness as a healer lies within your ability to decide where your healee is open to receive a cleaning and balancing of their energy, and to be powerful enough to give them an empirical understanding of how whole health feels during the healing.

PROFESSIONAL ETHICS FOR HEALING

As with your code of ethics for reading another, the other's freedom and autonomy is of your highest concern. Never give a healing unless you have the other's permission. Although the Heartsong code of ethics is appropriate here also, you want to find a shorter version for actual use during the healing.

#124 EXERCISE
Purifying Yourself to Give a Healing

This exercise can be done either seated or standing.
Close your eyes.
Be in the center of your heart.
From that point of original essence energy deep in
  your Heart Chakra pull out your purest desire
  to be a clear channel and desire to give your
  healee exactly what they want and need for
  whole health... allow this energy to expand out
  into every cell in your Body... in this way you
  are setting your energy for the healing. This is
  called your Healing Prayer.
Be in the center of your head.
Come out of trance.
Bend over.

METHODS OF HEALING

There are several methods for healing another. The decision as to which method to use is based on your healee's receptivity to the healing and their *openings*. The opening is the picture or spot in the Auric Boundary where when touched automatically opens up your healee's energy Body. During the healing you may use one or several methods combined.

#125 EXERCISE   Cosmic energy . . . light orange
How to Find Your   Earth energy . . . light orange
    Healee's Openings

Sit in a trance position.

Close your eyes.

Be in the center of your head.

Go into trance.

Ground yourself.

Run your energy.

Look at your healee's Auric Boundary... there will be a spot that will light up... that is the opening.... it is to this point you begin a nonverbal communication with your healee... within a cord from your Throat Chakra to the same Chakra of your healee, throw the message, *"What method of healing will be in*

harmony with you?"... as your question hits the opening your answer will appear.
Be in the center of your own head.
Come out of trance.
Bend over.

BREATH AND RHYTHM

You may use both your *breath and rhythm* to join with your healee, or to set a balance of intake and out-take for your healee. Both you and your healee will find breath and rhythm a very relaxing experience.

#126 EXERCISE   Cosmic energy...light green
Breath and Rhythm   Earth energy...pink

Sit opposite each other in your trance positions.
As you inhale, the other exhales.
As you exhale, the other inhales.
Maintaining this breathing pattern together, neither person leading, both are following each other, for five to ten minutes.
Be in the center of your head.
Come out of trance.
Bend over.

VISUALIZATION

The only time that *visualization* will work is when you as a healer have the ability to throw a strong enough picture for it to be "seen" by your healee. Usually it will be a picture of the other in whole health, or possibly a more specific area of the Body being in vibrant health.

#127 EXERCISE
Image Healing

Cosmic energy... blue
Earth energy... blue

Sit in a trance position opposite your healee.

Close your eyes.

Be in the center of your head.

Go into trance.

Run your energy.

Get a really clear picture of your healee in total, full, whole health... when the image is very strong hold it up to show your healee... after you have held it up in front of you for a few minutes throw it to your healee's Sixth Chakra and let go of it.

Be in the center of your head.

Come out of trance.

Bend over.

CHANNELLING

Channelling energy means that the energy is running through your energy channels. You need a fair amount of clarity of who you are when you channel because the energy that runs through you is not yours. You use the energy that belongs to your healee. Your clarity, neutrality and grounding cord will protect you. You can either channel the energy actually through your personal energy channels, or you can channel it through only your Hand Chakras.

#128 EXERCISE   Energy...gold
Channelling Through Your Hand Chakras

Seat your healee in the trance position.
Stand behind your healee and place your hands palms down over your healee's Seventh Chakra ... postulate that your Hand Chakras are open, not only the Chakra in the palm of your hand but also on the backs of your hands... wide open right through your hands and into the crown of your healee's head... for this exercise you will channel the healee's highest level of creativity... right through your hands and into your healee's energy system... after several minutes of this, pull yourself back and flick off from your hands any energy that is caught there.
Be in the center of your head.
Bend over.
Come out of trance.

#129 EXERCISE
Color Healing

Seat your healee in the trance position.

Stand behind your healee and place your hands palm down over the Seventh Chakra... open your Hand Chakras.

Choose an appropriate color and bring in your Earth energy through your feet and your Cosmic energy through your Seventh Chakra ... mix these two energies in your pelvic cradle... channel them up your back channels up to your Heart Chakra... here you channel the energy down your arms and out your Hand Chakras... and into the Seventh Chakra of your healee... fill your healee up with the energy that you have chosen... allow all the energy that does not belong to your healee to go down *their* grounding cord.

End your healing.

Be in the center of your head.

Come out of trance.

Bend over.

#130 EXERCISE
"Toning-Up" Another's Chakras

Cosmic energy... peach
Earth energy... peach

Sit opposite your healee, both in your trance
    positions.
Close your eyes.
Be in the center of your heart.
Go into trance.
Bring your Earth energy and your Cosmic energy
    into your pelvic cradle... allow this mixed
    energy to flow up your back channels... open
    your Throat Chakra and channel the energy out
    your Throat Chakra... allow the energy to form
    tones and sounds... Start at the First Chakra
    and channel tones into your healee's First
    Chakra... still channelling the healing energy
    through your Throat Chakra, send several tones
    to each of the Seven Body Chakras.
End the channelling.
Be in the center of your own head.
Come out of trance.
Bend over.

#131 EXERCISE
Unconditional Love
And Acceptance

Cosmic energy... pink
Earth energy... pink

Sit in your trance position opposite your healee.
Close your eyes.
Be in the center of your heart.
Go into trance.
Pull in your Earth and Cosmic energies and mix
   them... send these energies up your back
   spine... open your Heart Chakra and send a
   cord to your healee's Heart Chakra... allow
   this energy to channel through the cord as ac-
   ceptance and love without conditions...
Cut the cord and end the healing.
Be in the center of your head.
Come out of trance.
Bend over.

OUT OF BODY HEALING

There are two types of *out-of-Body* healing. One is long distance healing. You Astrally project yourself to a person who is some distance away, and while you are out of your Body your Astral Body heals that person. The other is when your Astral Body becomes very small and you project yourself into the energy Body of your healee.

#132 EXERCISE   Cosmic energy...lavender
Long Distance   Earth energy...light green
  Healing

Sit in your trance position.
Close your eyes.
Be in the center of your head.
Go into trance.
Run your energy.
Choose a person who has asked for healing from
    you... postulate that you are leaving your
    Body to visit this person... when you get there,
    ask if they would like a healing... with the go
    ahead, give this person a healing... end the
    healing.
Be back in the center of your head.
BE YOURSELF.
Come out of trance.
Bend over.

#133 EXERCISE
Out of Body Healing

Cosmic energy... yellow
Earth energy... light green

Sit in your trance position opposite your healee.

Cose your eyes.

Be in the center of your head.

Go into trance.

Run your energy.

Leave your Body from the Crown of your head...
be sure you have a silver cord attached between
the physical Body and Astral Body... enter your
healee's Body through their Crown Chakra...
by allowing yourself to be very small, you can go
into the energy system through the channels and
actually into the Chakras to loosen and mend
energy patterns. The Wilderness back-packing
rule applies here: *take nothing, leave nothing*.
You are there to correct faulty energy patterns,
yet you leave none of yourself, and take none of
the healee when you are gone... leave the
healee's Body the same way you entered...
through the Crown Chakra.

Be in the center of your head.

Pull all of yourself into the center of your head.

Come out of trance.

Bend over.

HOW TO GIVE A HEALING

Now that you have learned some methods of healing, you are ready for some guidelines to remember while you are healing. These guidelines will give your Healing a professional attitude which you will find is a comfort to your Healee.

1. Before you enter the Healing room, look at yourself... where are you? Who are you?
2. Leave your problems and projections outside of the healing room.
3. Sit opposite the healee.
4. Introduce yourself and explain healing procedures.
5. Go into trance, setting your color a few shades lighter than the Healee... this way you can read and heal without becoming their problems or personality patterns.
6. Ground yourself.
7. Clean yourself out.
8. Ground the Healee.
9. Ground the room.
10. From a light trance state, ask the Healee to speak of the nature of the problem... as the Healee answers, listen to both the physical words and the astral words...
11. When reading the problem, approach the healee's energy as a whole seeking out the energy patterns that support the problem.
12. Evaluate the energy problem and decide what form of healing you will use... out of body... channelling color, tones... etc....
13. Explain to the Healee what you see and what you will be doing.
14. State your Healing Prayer to yourself.
15. Do the Healing.
16. Make a separation.
17. Clean yourself out... remove cords, blow matching or/and stuck pictures, be in the center of your head and be yourself.
18. Clean out the room.
19. Come out of trance.
20. Bend over, and let go of the healing.

Chapter Ten

CREATING SHARED REALITIES

CO-CREATION

HOW TO CO-CREATE A PARTNERSHIP

HOW TO CO-CREATE A SHARED
REALITY: GROUP REALITY

CO-CREATION

Every particle of energy in the Universe is within the shared Collective Reality. Whether it is as close to you as your family and home, or as far away as the Moon, these people, places and things are all ultimately within your daily life, with or without your awareness of them. Your energy overlaps, combines, and unites with the energies of all others. By common agreement, these collective energies synthesize into the realities that you experience every day. Together we create and manifest the chairs, tables, books, food, cars, houses, and all that we have in our shared Collective Reality.

Your ability to consciously influence this shared space develops in direct proportion with your ability both to know yourself and to surrender that self to the specific creation of which you are part. When you know who you are and who you are not, you are not sidetracked by mistaken responsibilities. Instead you are able to recognize, handle, create and manifest your energy within the context of your fullest potential. You take on only your part, and you allow others their part. Whether you are one with one other, one within a group or one within the WHOLE (ALL THAT IS)—whether you are a follower or a leader, no matter how large or small your part appears—your part, each part, everyone's part, is of equal importance. It is the pulling together of the group energy and the mutual surrender to the evolution of the common goal that directly influences your ability to manifest lasting creations together. The more consciously each does their part, the more evolved the "WHOLE" will be.

HOW TO CO-CREATE A PARTNERSHIP

The two following exercises will enable you to both create your relationship contract and to continuously keep your relationship *co-created*. The relationship contract is to the relationship as the skeleton is to the Human Body. Within this analogy you would liken the relationship itself to the rest of the Human Body.

#134 EXERCISE
How to Consciously
Create a Relationship Contract

Cosmic energy... pink
Earth energy... light green

You and the other sit directly across from each
other.

Sit in your trance positions.

Both are to be in the center of your own heads.

Both are to ground themselves and ground the relationship.

Both are to go into trance.

Both are to run your own energy.

Both are to match the same color of energy, each
taking an equal part in the balancing and maintaining of this energy.

Both are to make an affinity connection with the
other (Heart Chakra cords).

Open your eyes and verbally talk, all the while
maintaining the balance of energy... Come to
some agreed upon conclusions as to the direction
and limits of the relationship.

Close your eyes and create an outline of a heart between you... Take the words, pictures, goals,
that describe the direction and limits of your relationship and throw this energy into the
heart...

A contract will form from the energy you both offer... Let go of the contract and send it to the
Akashic Records (Group Memory).

Be in the center of your own head.

BE YOURSELF.

Come out of trance.

Bend over.

#135 EXERCISE   Cosmic energy... light violet
How to Continuously   Earth energy... violet
  Create a Relationship

> You and the other sit directly across from each
>   other. Sit in your trance position, close enough
>   for your knees to touch the other.
> Close your eyes.
> Both are to be in the center of your own heads.
> Both are to ground yourselves and ground the re-
>   lationship.
> Both are to go into trance.
> Both are to run your own energy.
> Both match the same color of energy... each tak-
>   ing an equal part in the balancing of the energy
>   ... and take equal part in maintaining that
>   color.
> Both are to make a heart connection with the
>   other.
> Both are to go up to the Tenth and Eleventh
>   Chakras (Probable and Possible Universes) and
>   get a clear idea or picture of what you personal-
>   ly want... Both are to pull the picture down in-
>   to your Seventh Chakras, and know it... your
>   Sixth Chakras and get a clear picture of your
>   own responsibility to attain that picture... and
>   into both Fifth Chakras... and talk about...
>   both explaining the pictures with words and us-
>   ing Sixth Chakra projection to project a clear

picture of what you are saying to the other...
each taking an equal turn and coming to a con-
clusion, or mutually agreed-upon goal... Pull
that goal into their Heart Chakras to be in affinity with it, and into the Third Chakra to
distribute a copy of the goal into every cell of
your Body...then project the goal out from
every cell in your Body.

every cell in your Body.

Be in the center of your own heads.

BE YOURSELVES.

Come out of trance.

Bend over.

Verbally communicate what you experienced
with each other.

HOW TO CO-CREATE WITHIN A GROUP

By dropping all personal ego, needs, and wants, the whole of the group becomes the major goal. With this in mind, the following exercise will enable you to work together as if your collective Souls were ONE.

#136 EXERCISE
How to Co-Create
A Group Reality

Cosmic energy... light violet
Earth energy... violet

Sit your group in a circle, each member in their
trance position.

Each is to be in the center of their own head.

Each is to go into trance.

Each is to ground themself, and to ground the
room.

The leader is to run the appropriate color of energy, and as the excess flows from the Crown,
fill up the entire room with that color.

Each member is to match the color of that energy
from their own space.

Each member is to balance their own energy and
take an equal part in holding the color in the
room.

Each member is to go into either their upper
Tenth (Probable Universe) or the Eleventh
(Possible Universe), and get a clear idea of the
mutually agreed-upon goal... Keep that idea
well defined and clear... and then go into the
lower Tenth or Eleventh Chakra and get a well
defined, clear image of the goal... Then each
member is to project that image outwards from
both their upper and lower centers in all directions around them... until the images from the
upper and lower Chakras meet... each

member taking responsibility for projecting and holding the goal in their own Reality Aura.

Each is to look at the goal to be achieved and to decide upon their own personal part in its creation.

Each is to pull their own part into the Crown of their heads and know it.

Then each is to pull it into the Sixth Chakra and see it, getting a clear understanding of their own personal part.

Each is to pull it into the Fifth Chakra and speak to it, making their own part into a clear affirmation (positive statement).

Each is to pull their own part into the Heart Chakra and to be at one with it.

Each is to pull their part into the Third Chakra, and from there distribute it into every cell in their bodies.

At this point, each is to take absolute responsibility for their own part and to project it out from every cell in their bodies until it meets the common goal that has been projected from the Upper and Lower Chakras...

Each is to be in the center of their own head.

All come out of trance.

Bend over.

Chapter Eleven

WE CAN MAKE A DIFFERENCE BY WORKING TOGETHER

YOUR PART

HEART CONNECTION WITH
EVERYONE

PEACE NOW

THE CIRCLE OF HUMANKIND

WE CAN MAKE A DIFFERENCE
BY WORKING TOGETHER

Every Friday evening between 7:00 and 8:30 Heartsong School conducts a free Healing Circle. This is our service for the public community. The Healing Circle offers individual healings, group healings and guided pro-evolutionary meditations. The meditations are designed to enhance the quality of life for all by unifying the planet and the peoples on it as *ONE HUMANKIND*.

Group energy is a very powerful tool. Your assistance in this group effort would help greatly! Whether you are at Heartsong on any Friday evening or are at home, please join us for a time of unity.

#137 EXERCISE
Your Part

Cosmic energy... gold
Earth energy... silver

Sit in your trance position.

Close your eyes.

Be in the center of your head.

Go into trance.

Ground yourself.

Run your energy.

Postualte that the WHOLE (ALL THAT IS) is a very large Body... and that you are one cell in that Body of GOD... What cell would you be?... Where would you be located?... What would be your functions to maintain the WHOLE?...

Surrender to the unity of the WHOLE...

Be your part.

Be in the center of your head.

Come out of trance.

Bend over.

#138 EXERCISE
Heart Connection
  With Everyone

Cosmic energy... pink gold
Earth energy... pink

Sit in your trance position.

Close your eyes.

Be in the center of your head.

Go into trance.

Ground yourself.

Run your energy.

Take a cord of energy from your Heart Chakra and make a connection with the ones you love the most... Now throw a Heart Cord to everyone else: Throw a cord to the people you see in your every day life... the people you work with... the people in your neighborhood... Consciously make a connection to everyone in the city that you live in... and in the State you live in... Now make a Heart Connection to everyone in the Country that you live... and the Countries that surround your Country... Make a Heart Connection to every person in your Hemisphere... and in all the cities, States, and Countries in the other Hemisphere... Make a strong Heart Cord to every Soul on the Planet Earth... *ONE HUMAN-KIND... ONE PEOPLE... ONE WORLD*.

Be in the center of your head.

BE YOURSELF and part of the WHOLE at the same time.

Come out of trance.

Bend over.

#139 EXERCISE
Peace Now

Cosmic energy... silver
Earth energy... copper

Sit in your trance position.
Close your eyes.
Be in the center of your head.
Go into trance.
Ground yourself.
Run your energy.
Go up to your Eleventh or Tenth Chakras (Probable and Possible Universes) and envision a
World without War... a World where there is
no division caused by the resistance of in-
dividual egos... a World where the common
good of All has importance... a World where
people share themselves, yet each takes total
responsibility for themselves... a World that
protects life and enhances the quality of that
life... Notice the Spiritual Matter that is needed to make up this vision.
Go down to your lower Eleventh and Tenth
Chakras and envision this same peaceful
World here... where we are all ONE HU-
MANKIND... Notice the physical matter
needed to make up this vision.
Project the vision from the lower and upper
Chakras in all directions around you... until
the lower and upper images meet and synthesize...

Notice your part... Get a clear image of your
part... Be in affinity with your part... Pull it
into both the Crown of your head and into
your feet... and run the energy of your part
through your energy channels, and feed your
Aura, your Chakras and every cell in your
Body with your part... BE YOUR PART...
Allow every cell in your Body to be your
part...

Be in the center of your head.

Come out of trance.

Bend over.

#140 EXERCISE
The Circle of Humankind

Cosmic energy... gold
Earth energy... gold

Sit in your trance position.

Close your eyes.

Be in the center of your head.

Go into trance.

Ground yourself.

Run your energy.

Postulate that you are within a circle and invite your family and friends to enter it... now invite all the people that you work with into the circle... and then all your neighbors... allow and invite everyone in your city to be in this circle with you... invite everyone in your state to be within the circle... invite everyone that lives within your country to be within the circle with you... everyone in your hemisphere... everyone on the planet Earth... allow the circle to include every being on the planet Earth... *ONE HUMANKIND.*

Be in the center of your head.

Come out of trance.

Bend over.

AFTERWORD

The importance of the experience and re-experience of actually doing the exercises in this book can not be stressed enough. When you are done with **OPENING-UP**, go through it again and redo the exercises that are the hardest for you. Restudy the concepts that are the most confusing to you. Blow up any and all pictures that come between you and your clarity. Repeat the creative exercises until you are able to manifest your creations. It took you a long time to close down, burdened by energy that belongs to others and burdened by your own overly charged pictures. You can expect to take a while to open up and reacquaint you with yourself. Your perseverance will be rewarded with the newfound intimacies and love you will have within yourself and for others... and of course the clarity of consciousness that you will have from seeing clearly.

If this book initiates any question, comments, or experiences that you wish to share with me, please feel free to write me:

Petey Stevens
P.O. Box 9779
Berkeley, California 94709

or call me at Heartsong:
415-527-4833

GLOSSARY

A

abilities: that which you are able to do

affinity: to be at one with

affirmation: to state as if a fact, a positive declaration

Akashic Records: Group Memory

astral projection: when the Soul leaves the physical Body either in the Past, Present or Future or into the Astral Planes

autonomy: self governing, functioning and acting without the control of others

Aura: a field of energy that surrounds and emanates from the Human Body

B

block: an interruption, restraining or halting of the energy flow

boundaries: the outer edge of your Aura where you end and the rest of the world begins

C

certainty: the ability to be sure of yourself

Chakra: an energy center in your personal energy system that transmits and receives energy messages

channels: natural vibratory linkage or pathways between points of consciousness

charge: emotional trauma

circuitry: energy hook-ups

clairsentience: the ability to feel another's emotion

clearing: to rid yourself of energy that controls you

co-creation: to create with another or others

compassion: to understand another through affinity

consciousness: the part of you that is aware

contract: agreement

Cosmic: the energy that makes up the Universe exclusive of the Planet Earth and other planetary bodies

cords: communication lines between individuals

crack: the first show of release of blocked or frozen energy

D

dichotomies: two sides of an issue locked in relationship

disembodied: a Soul that is not connected to a Body

E

elements: most basic particles that create the Universe

energy: that essence of which all things are made

energy system: the totality of you on an energy level; Soul, grounding cord, circuitry, channels, Aura, Chakras

empathy: to take into yourself and reflect back to them another's emotions

F

frozen energy: energy that is still transparent yet held still in one place

G

Genetic Key: genetic programming

H

havingness: the ability to have or receive

healing: to make whole

hole: a gap in the Aura

I

"in the Body": the Soul is in the physical Body

intuition: direct knowing without using reason

K

Karma: the law of cause and effect

Kundalini: the mixture of Earth and Cosmic energies

M

machine: a formation of energy that acts as a slide projector, projecting a certain picture or set of pictures in front of you

manifest: to make real, to bring into the physical plane

mask: an energy disguise in the outer layer of the Aura

matching: the same as

merging: combining the energy of two or more Auras into one Aura.

mock-up: a postulated image

multi-dimensional: many dimensions (measurements) in one Universe or one consciousness

N

nonresistance: to allow to pass through

O

open: receptive

opening: the picture that is open to a Healing or Reading

original essence energy: the energy of who you really are (or were at the first moment that your Soul came into existance)

"out of Body": when the Soul is not in the Body

P

picture: energy formation which carries information on a psychic level

postulate: to imagine as if real

power: the energy to manifest

programming: energy patterns which control you

psychic: of the Soul

psychic opening: becoming aware of who you are

R

reading: to look at and translate energy patterns

reality: that which is real or exists according to the observer

resistance: to be against

running energy: channelling both Earth and Cosmic energy through your Body

S

screen: a method of blocking out certain energies and allowing other energies in

seniority: the ability to be in charge or have the final say when it comes to your own Body

shield: a method of blocking out all energy or awareness
Spirit Eye: the Sixth Chakra, the Third Eye
stuck: a constant perpetuation of a rigid pattern of behavior
symbol: metaphor
sympathy: to feel and take on another's emotion

T

telekinesis: the ability to move an object with your mind
telepathy: to send and/or receive thoughts
trance: to transcend or move through one dimension of yourself to another dimension of yourself
transcend: to go beyond

V

valence: to become the other's personality pattern
vibration: the movement of energy

W

whack: a negative energy communication, an insult

325

EXERCISES

329